CRASH GO THE CHARIOTS

CHARIOTS

Revised and Enlarged

Clifford Wilson

MASTER BOOKS

ISBN: 0-89051-023-7

Library of Congress
Card Catalog Number 76-20176

Copyright © 1976

MASTER BOOKS, A Division of CLP
San Diego, California 92115

An Explanation

Three years have passed since *Crash Go The Chariots* was first published in the United States. The book quickly became a best seller; but then the American publishers (Lancer Books) got into financial difficulties and for some time the book was frozen. Now the time of the original contract has expired and it can be released again.

It has been revised and updated, with additional material added at appropriate points. We have avoided intruding on the new material covered by *The Chariots Still Crash*, a sequel to *Crash Go The Chariots*, put out by New American Library (Signet Books). Thus, in this volume, we do not touch on such matters as Erich von Daniken's Gold of the Gods which is dealt with in *The Chariots Still Crash*.

An additional chapter has been added dealing with the Bermuda Triangle. Since entering this debate with *Crash Go The Chariots*, it has constantly been driven home to me that there is a great public interest in this seemingly mysterious area. Hence the new material.

Crash Go The Chariots is re-issued because of the continuing interest in this subject. Hopefully, *Crash Go The Chariots* will be of interest to many who have been caused to wonder about visits of astronauts from outer space, and various unexplained mysteries around the world. We do not claim to answer all the problems, but we do claim to show that as knowledge increases, so-called mysteries are explainable after all. This applies equally to von Daniken's theories and to the wild conjectures of various writers about the Bermuda Triangle.

17553

CONTENTS

1

WATCH OUT FOR
THOSE ARCHAEOLOGISTS!

In his *Chariots of the Gods?* Erich von Daniken makes statements about archaeologists and archaeology that are quite without foundation, and are often factually in gross error. He states:

> Scholars make things very easy for themselves. They stick a couple of old potsherds together, search for one or two adjacent cultures, stick a label on the restored find and — hey presto! — once again everything fits splendidly into the approved pattern of thought. (Page 37, *Chariots of the Gods?*, 2nd Australian edition.)

Is he serious? At first as I read *Chariots of the Gods?* I could not believe that some of his wild statements were meant to be taken seriously; but as I read on and came across large numbers of unsupported conjectures, I realized that at least many of his readers would consider that Erich von Daniken is very much in earnest in his criticisms of scholars in the field of archaeology. According to von Daniken, they "fit into the approved pattern of thought," for this is in their own interests, and this "is obviously very much simpler than chancing the idea that an embarrassing technical skill might have existed, or the thought of space travellers in the distant past. That would be complicating matters unnecessarily."

Such statements are outlandish, as are so many of von Daniken's comments. Their challenge against scholars who are doing first-class work in their comparatively new science demands an answer; to some extent that answer is presented in these pages. The attempt is by no means complete, for von Daniken touches on so many areas that it would take a much larger volume than is here intended to answer all the points he raises.

It is not for a moment denied that some of the points he raises are fascinating and thought-provoking. In a radio debate with this author in Melbourne, Australia, he made the point that many of his arguments were put out to be provocative. It would be an understatement to say that he has at least achieved that objective!

Von Daniken seems to take special delight in attacking archaeologists. He sees a need for panels of experts to replace "archaeologists" as they are thought of today.

My own experience is that archaeological teams are NOT as limited as von Daniken suggests. This was illustrated at Tell Gezer, in Israel, where I was an Area Supervisor.

Experts From Many Fields

The team of excavators included world famous names such as Nelson Glueck, G. Ernest Wright, and William Dever. The list of Field and Area Supervisors read somewhat like a miniature

"Who's Who" in archaeology. The team also included scholars from other disciplines that were seemingly as widely separated as Geology, History, and Theology.

They came from radically different backgrounds and from differing religious persuasions. There were Protestants, Roman Catholics, Jews, and agnostics. Some had a special respect for the Bible while others rejected the spiritual tone it demanded.

It was fascinating to listen to men who differed so radically in many ways, as they discussed the finds of that particular day analyzing, reconstructing, suggesting, opposing a viewpoint, and agreeing to a new approach where the facts demanded it.

One point that I am especially stressing is that these men were experts. They took their work extremely seriously as they made chemical tests, sifted (literally and figuratively) the evidence, pored over many cross-referencing texts, compared pottery and other finds with similar artifacts from sites near and far, meticulously recorded every aspect of the excavations, and ensured that professional photographs were taken as the excavations proceeded in the various areas of the dig. There were collapsible steps to ensure that photographs could be taken from a height, and there was even a collapsible tower which was moved from area to area as required. The Director of the excavation even utilized a helicopter to ensure that comprehensive aerial photographs of the best quality were taken.

Archaeologists Face the Facts

There were experts in History and Archaeology, men with hard-earned Ph.D.s from top Universities. They specialized in various archaeological time periods, from the bronze age to relatively modern times.

I certainly did not gain the impression that they were inflexible or unwilling to adjust to new facts. I listened to, and participated in, discussions as to whether a building should be dated to Solomonic or Maccabean times, or whether a cache of Philistine pots could be fitted into accepted chronological dating for pottery remains. Visits were made to various sites to compare findings, and to seek the opinions of scholars actively engaged in other relevant excavations.

We see, then, that archaeology is not a discipline consisting only of experts in one particular academic area. Experts in different ancient languages, pottery conservationists, a doctor, theologians of world standing, and experts in other disciplines, were at Gezer. They reported for duty at sunrise, and often finished off their reports about midnight.

They came from many parts of the world, and included an Irish architect-surveyor. Some of the Americans found him even harder to understand than me, with my Australian accent! There was some compensation on that point, for Professor Nelson Glueck told me he liked to talk to me, just to hear my accent. It reminded him of the late Alan Rowe, with whom he had excavated at Beth Shan many years before.

The point I am making is that these men were experts in various fields, ready to listen and to adapt. They were true scholars, and would look the evidence squarely in the face, even when it seemed to prove them wrong.

Possibly one of the best examples of that was the late Professor William Foxwell Albright, probably the greatest archaeologist and expert in ancient languages that the world has ever seen, or ever will see. He was not at the excavation of Gezer, but soon afterwards I had a long conversation with him, stretching over several hours, at his home in Baltimore. Part of the time we spent at the nearby Johns Hopkins University where we had lunch and entered into conversation with some of those who now sat where he had sat (he was Professor Emeritus). In much of that discussion I felt like a small boy in the presence of a mental giant, for Dr. Albright moved from Accadian to Egyptian hieroglyphics, and to various other ancient languages as he entered with gusto into the topic under discussion.

However it was by no means one-sided. He listened to the opinions of others, ready to concede points as the evidence demanded. It was stimulating to see, and to be the guest of such a man. In a further private conversation afterwards we discussed many of the controversial points of archaeology, and it was again refreshing to realize that this great man had been prepared to change his mind time and time again over the years. He readily acknowledged that some of his earlier tentative hypotheses had not always stood the test of later investigation.

It has sometimes been said that Professor Albright showed two faces in his writings. A person reading the first edition of *From the Stone Age to Christianity* would hardly recognize that this was the same author who just a few years later presented *The Biblical Period—From Abraham to Ezra*. The earlier writing showed only limited respect for the authenticity of the sacred historical record, while the latter pointed to the need for a return to a position closely resembling the orthodoxy of a previous day, as he put it.

Here was yet another archaeologist (recognized by many as the greatest of all time) freely changing course when the facts demanded it. This argument could be greatly extended, in such areas as the date of the excavated buildings at Jericho, the so-called "stables" at Megiddo, the nature of the buildings first wrongly thought to be furances at Ezion-Geber, and many others.

Von Daniken's Opinion of Archaeologists

Against this sort of evidence it is highly relevant to consider the viewpoints of Erich von Daniken. A typical statement is found in the second sentence of his introduction:

> Because its (the book's) theories and proofs do not fit into the mosaic of traditional archaeology, constructed so laboriously and firmly cemented down, scholars will call it nonsense . . . .

In the very next paragraph he goes on:

> Nevertheless one thing is certain. There is something inconsistent about our past, that past which lies thousands and millions of years behind us. The past teemed with unknown gods who visited the primeval earth in manned space-ships.

Over and over again von Daniken does not substantiate his arguments, and opinions and conclusions are built very quickly on suppositions for which there is no convincing argument according to the normal demands of evidence. Archaeologists are NOT limited to theories that are, as von Daniken states, "laboriously and firmly cemented down," but in fact there are very many cases where they have revised their hypotheses when the evidence has so demanded.

That Airfield at Nazca in Peru

One of the clear examples of Erich von Daniken's writing against archaeologists relates to those mysterious lines near the ancient city of Nazca in Peru. He tells of gigantic lines that run parallel to each other, and then comments:

The archaeologists say that they are Inca roads. A preposterous idea! What use were roads that run parallel to each other to the Incas? That intersect? That are laid out in a plain and come to a sudden end? (p.31).

So the archaeologists are foolish, and the correct answer, according to the author of *Chariots of the Gods?*, in his own words, is as follows:

Seen from the air, the clear-cut impression that the 37-mile-long plain of Nazca made on me was that of an airfield. (p. 32).

He goes on to say that to classical archaeology "the theory that aircraft could have existed in antiquity is sheer humbug."

As one looks at statements like this there are glaring errors, and we shall consider the case of the Nazca airfield as our first examination of Von Daniken's hypotheses.

The Case of the Airfield at Nazca

In the above quotation, von Daniken suggests that "seen from the air" the impression is gained that the Nazca Plain was an airfield. He even goes on to ask, "What is so far-fetched about the idea?" Most of those Nazca lines are about four inches wide, and they certainly could not mark out the landing field of an airport. Some wider lines go for quite short distances, up to about 300 feet in length.

In olden times the people cleared away the stones and the dirt, and piled up stones at the side of the field. They then packed down the dirt on the Plain itself and mixed in some sort of powder with it. The surface of the plain itself is very hard, for only about half an inch of rain falls each year in this desert area; it is the driest desert in the world.

The stones are quite small; they are not even big enough to prevent cars driving across the desert. In *Chariots of the Gods?* there is a picture of a supposed parking area at this "airport" on the Nazca

Plain, and some of the stones are there. Calculating from their size, von Daniken's "parking area" would be only about three or four feet across, and that refers to the whole area of double lines which supposedly make up von Daniken's "parking area."

The lines themselves are quite shallow, being about half an inch to an inch in depth, and certainly they do not represent something on which spacecraft would land.

In addition to these impacted lines, there are many tracks of cars and trucks, and even of military vehicles; there is virtually no rain to wash them away.

Von Daniken suggests that it is a preposterous suggestion on the part of the archaeologists to claim that these lines are Inca roads. He does not, however, state which archaeologist suggests they are roads. It is a fact that properly formed Inca roads run all through the Andes, but these lines on the Nazca Plain have nothing to do with those roads. Anybody seeing them from the ground would immediately concede that point. The famous Inca roads that ran all through the Andes Mountains helped to give cohesion to the Inca Empire. Such far-reaching roads were built by thousands of slaves, and certainly astronauts were not brought in to help. The roads were usually some three meters in width and extended over about a thousand miles. These roads extend through such South American countries as Ecuador, Bolivia, and Chile, as well as Peru. Some are still being used today.

Road Building by the Mayas

Although it is nonsense to suggest that the Nazca lines were part of an airfield, in that same context von Daniken writes about the marvels of the middle American culture of the Mayas, which in many ways is comparable. Strictly speaking, this is another topic; but I shall touch on it because of its relevance to Erich von Daniken's suggestion that it is "a preposterous idea" to suggest that what he refers to as roads "laid out geometrically" "are Inca roads." The Mayas, to whom von Daniken refers in this connection, were actually inferior to the Incas and to the Nazca people. Thus it is especially interesting to notice the comments of the archaeologist J. Eric S. Thompson about some of the Mayan roads:

> The building of these roads entailed tremendous labor and not a little engineering knowledge. In swampy sections, the engineers had to be sure that their foundations were deep and secure (there are no detours to avoid swampy sections); the lack of any evidence of subsidence demonstrates that they solved the problem. The tracing of the routes must have presented problems, too. The road from Coba to Yaxuna follows these directions: start to mile 4, 279°; mile 4 to mile 10, 269°; mile 10 to mile 15, 260°; mile 15 to mile 20, 270°; mile 20 to mile 40, 260°; mile 40 to mile 62 (Yaxuna), 264° . . . there are two sections of twenty and twenty-two miles respectively without any change of direction. *(The Rise and Fall of Maya Civilization*, p. 186.)*

He goes on to point out that this was a very difficult task, with the forest all around the engineer. Elsewhere (p.75) he refers to an "elaborate network of roads" connecting these cities, and refers to side roads leading to old ruins (p. 186).

It is also relevant to comment that it takes only a few years for such roads to be completely covered by the thick forest vegetation. Thompson tells how at Tikal it was necessary for archaeologists to re-clear the forest from the ruins in 1881, 1904, and 1910 because each time the "vegetation had engulfed the ruins anew" (p.7).

He points out that the Mayas were inferior to the Aztecs in road building (p. 185), and it is therefore hard to see why von Daniken should argue against the possibility of geometric patterns in old South American roads. There is clear geometric pattern shown in the quotation above, and the description indicates that remarkable roads were built by people whose achievements were inferior to those of the Nazca people to whom von Daniken refers.

Roads for "Non-practical" Religious Purposes

The Mayan roads were not built for practical purposes, for the Mayas had no beasts of burden or wheeled vehicles. Rather, it seems that they were for spiritual purposes — Thompson suggests they were utilized "as a setting for great religious processions" (p.189).

He goes on to say that even the corbelled vault would not be employed for utilitarian purposes, but as an embodiment of sacrificial effort. He also tells (p. 185) of a platform 40 feet long and over 16 feet high that covers the road, just before it reaches the outer suburbs of Coba, and it is probable that processions halted at this point to make sacrifices before continuing on into the city.

It is generally believed that the people in South America did not utilize the wheel to any great extent. They certainly knew about it, for some have been found in tombs at various centers. Probably Inca and other South American roads were built so that the points of the Empire could be connected, and also so that sacrificial processions could be undertaken at regular intervals.

Helping the Gods to Land

If these people at Nazca were expecting their gods to return, why would they need a new landing ground anyway? Why did they not come in the same way as on the first visit? Then it is reasonable to ask, "Would those 'astronauts' land in airplanes — surely they would come in spaceships?" In either case, why would they need landing strips extending over 37 miles, the figure which von Daniken gives?

In any case, if the landing strips at Nazca are simply earth, one inch deep, and not rock or modern concrete, would not the jet-stream of supposed spacecraft blast them away, leaving no trace? In fact, would not they blast huge holes wherever they did land? Those amazing engineers — amazing by von Daniken's own statements — would certainly not have made earth landing strips. We could also ask what sort of braking systems the spaceships must have had, apparently requiring many miles of landing strip to be effective.

There Is No Pre-Historic Airfield in the Andes

Those Nazca lines extend over three separate areas that are divided by valleys, with quite a deep valley running down between the separate areas where the lines are found. No aircraft, ancient or modern, could land in these areas of steep ravines.

The Views of Maria Reiche

Archaeologists tend to believe that the "original" lines (not the modern ones made by cars, etc.) were astronomical and calendrical in nature; this view is especially supported by the German scientist Maria Reiche who has lived in Nazca for some 20 years. She believes that geometrical principles were implemented in the construction of these huge figures in the desert, utilizing pivot rocks and long cords. In *Time* magazine of 30th March, 1974, she showed how this apparently was undertaken. Alongside some of the huge figures there are miniatures of the same drawings, in plots about six feet square. These were drawn out on a much larger scale by using cords, producing the etchings that are now found on the Nazca Plain. Some of the pivot stones and markings are still in position, and on some of the plots small editions of the larger etchings can be seen.

The Inca people co-ordinated the angles and curves that were necessary to draw these huge figures of birds, animals, constellations, and so on. Actually you cannot even see the end of some of the figures from the ground, for hills and other natural features intrude. At times they run right over a hill and down a valley they could hardly have been drawn without some plan such as Maria Reiche suggests.

The people of Peru were animists and worshipped all sorts of things on the ground around them and in the heavens above.

Even that huge trident on the mountain, to which von Daniken refers, probably had religious significance. It has three separate lines, and is high up on the face of the cliff. Although opinions vary, it probably depicts a cactus plant, and it certainly looks like one of the many cactus plants that grow wild in the area. It gives the impression of being a single cactus having its main stalk running up, then having two branches that stretch out on either side. It has no leaves, and this is typical of many of the cacti in the general area of Nazca.

Another possibility is that these lines on the cliffs depict a candelabra. Professor Garcia Montero points out that the nearby Bay of Tisco was a known pirate haven, and he suggests that the pirates made this candlestick holder as a diversion. Its type path of construction is quite different from that of the Nazca lines. If this interpretation is correct, it would suggest a Catholic background. Either way, whether candelabra or cactus, the lines on the cliff would have religious significance.

Certainly the fact of this construction on the side of the cliff is not incredible and would not require astronaut help as von Daniken implies. There have been other famous carvings high up the sides of the mountains, such as those on the Behistun Rock, which tell of the achievements of the ancient Persian king, Darius the Great.

Ancient rulers built all sorts of monuments, and it is possible that this huge cliff drawing had something to do with the movements of heavenly bodies that were so important to all peoples in relation to the planting and harvesting of their crops. Many of these ancient people knew about equinoxes and solstices, and other supposedly "modern" concepts.

Thus it is possible that von Daniken's suggestion, that the figure on the cliff was drawn for someone to see from the air, is close to the truth. These people worshipped heavenly bodies such as the sun, the moon, and the stars; and it is entirely possible that Inca people drew this great trident on the cliff as an act of devotion to their gods. Very possibly there was some religious significance that we no longer understand.

As I have suggested, another interesting possibility is that some of the Nazca lines were tied in with astronomical and calendrical data. Local people now living at Nazca state that every two months a different line follows the path of the sun as it moves to the south and then to the north. It is certain that many of the fertility rites of the Incas were related to the planting of seeds and the time of ploughing. They were tied in with the calendar, and the Incas believed that heavenly bodies were important in their daily lives. They even had a tradition about tying the sun down, and this was actually at the time of the southern solstice. When the sun reached its furthest southern point they performed this rite, and even had "the hitching post of the sun" in their capital city, where they ceremonially tied the sun down on a certain day. Sure enough, the sun would then start moving north again, for they knew the right day for this ceremony.

Reverend Donald Bond, a Missionary who lives in Nazca, reported some of the above facts to me after he had read the earlier edition of *Crash Go The Chariots*, and he concluded on this note:

> Obviously these ancient people were capable of great achievements. However, what von Daniken says about the Nazca lines cannot be taken seriously. This makes me doubt his other conclusions also. I agree with you that his chariots still crash.

2

EASTER ISLAND, THE PYRAMIDS, AND EMBALMING

The Problem of Easter Island

To investigate one "mystery" we need to voyage to Easter Island, about 2,000 miles off the coast of Chile in the Pacific Ocean.

Here the author of *Chariots of the Gods?* has really let his imagination go in an attempt to bolster his theory of visitors from outer space. He tells us:

An orally transmitted legend tells us that flying men landed and lit fires in ancient times.

The legend is confirmed by sculptures of flying creatures with big staring eyes   (p. 115).

For the sake of the theory, it seems a pity that the legend was only orally transmitted. However, it is hardly convincing to say it is "confirmed" by the evidence of the flying creatures to which the author refers!

On this matter it is interesting to read in *Chariots* some of the results of Thor Heyerdahl's investigations: he is the man of *Kon-Tiki* fame.

Apparently, Heyerdahl's investigations were accepted as sufficient authority for *Chariots* at certain points, since von Daniken quotes him where it suits; but at other points of great importance Heyerdahl is either ignored or overlooked. Von Daniken tells of Heyerdahl discovering hundreds of unfinished statues and thousands of stone implements, including axes (p. 114), but then he goes off into his own theory:

> The usual explanation, that the stone giants were moved to their present sites on wooden rollers, is not feasible in this case, either . . . Then who cut the statues out of the rock, who carved them and transported them to their sites? How were they moved across country for miles without rollers? How were they dressed, polished and erected? How were the hats, the stone for which came from a different quarry from that of the statues, put in place? (p. 114).

Where do the two authors disagree? One point relates to the number of people who could have lived on the Island — von Daniken says 2,000 while Heyerdahl says about 7,000. According to von Daniken "2,000 men were not nearly enough to carve these colossal figures out of the steel-hard volcanic stone with rudimentary tools, even if they worked day and night" (p. 114). In direct contradiction, Heyerdahl suggests that only a few men would be needed to carve the great figures out of volcanic craters, making use of stone axes harder than the rock they were working on. Great quantities of suitable axes were actually found. Von Daniken himself acknowledges this at page 114, yet makes much of the supposed fact that this "steel-hard volcanic rock had been cut through like butter" and goes on to ask how the rock could be cut, dressed, and polished (pp. 114-115). The axes would have been used for flaking the rock, then dressing it. Easter Island itself gives this answer, clear to those with "eyes to see."

Von Daniken also sees it as an insuperable problem for the limited population to move the statues from their native rock sites to their new resting places some miles away; but the *Kon-Tiki* man has supplied the answer. He estimated that about a thousand men would have been required to pull the statues from the quarry site, but only about 500 men would have been needed to transport them to their new "home" where inclined ramps had previously been prepared. He demonstrated that the statues could have been dragged up feet first and toppled over into the prepared hole after which the "hat" of a different stone was dragged up the ramp and also placed in position. In passing, it is interesting to mention that not all writers agree that this second stone was a "hat," but suggest that it was supposed to represent hair. Most go along with the "hat" theory.

As we examine the evidence, the theories of Heyerdahl are supported rather than those of von Daniken. It is even acknowledged in *Chariots* that Heyerdahl discovered hundreds of unfinished statues on the island, and some of the old inclined ramps are still standing.

Aku-Aku, the Secret of Easter Island

The death-knell to von Daniken's hypothesis comes from another book by Thor Heyerdahl, *Aku-Aku, the Secret of Easter Island* (1958). It makes fascinating reading.

Three facets of particular interest relate to the commencement of a new Easter Island statue, to the re-erection of one of the fallen colossi, and to the actual movement of an Easter Island statue across the plain. They are told in continuous narrative form and are fascinating reading on pages 132 to 151 of *Aku-Aku*. Photographs are supplied in color, forever dispelling much of the mystery surrounding these famous old statues. Those photographs are irrefutable evidence demanding the rejection of von Daniken's hypothesis at this point.

A brief summary of the three stories follows:

On Easter Island, Thor Heyerdahl was told that the mayor was a member of the only family that was descended from the "long-ears" (their ears artifically made long), a group who had been responsible for the original statues. After Heyerdahl had made the right approaches, the mayor was released from his mayoral duties so that he and his relatives could carve a statue. The mayor's relatives were accepted as his co-workers because only descendants from the "long-ears" were eligible for this work.

Certain necessary religious ceremonies were undertaken, and then the work was commenced by six men, using abandoned stone picks which were in the quarry, "literally in hundreds" (p. 135).

A New Statue Takes Shape

Heyerdahl wrote:

Stroke followed stroke, the rock was hard; stone against stone, the little pick was the harder and the rock must give way. Clink-clink-clink, the blows of the picks must have been heard far out over the plain. For the first time in centuries the clink of stone was heard in Rano Raraku . . . .

Not much of a mark was made by each blow, hardly more than a grey patch of dust, but with another blow, and one more, and still another, something was gained. And at intervals the men grabbed the calabash and splashed water on the rock face, to soften it where they cut . . . ." (p. 136).

By the third day the contours of the newly created giant were "clearly visible on the rock wall." As a stone axe was blunted the mayor struck it against another on the ground, with splinters flaking off, "and he produced a new point as easily as a clerk sharpens a pencil" (p. 137). Heyerdahl goes on to tell that an average statue of fifteen feet high would require the services of about six men. The unfinished statues had been left because of technical flaws, such as a crack in the rock, and not because of lack of manpower.

The mayor estimated that it would take a year to complete the statue, which was longer than the visitors could allow, but the purpose of the exercise had been accomplished, for "the mayor and his men had now shown us the technique of the sculptors" (p. 137).

Von Daniken does not accept this verdict, and in *Return to the Stars* (pp. 128ff) he attempts to answer Thor Heyerdahl. However, he is unconvincing. "We, too, bashed away at the rock like wild men," he tells us, but after a few hundred blows "the rock showed hardly a scratch." In the same context (p. 125) he acknowledges that under Thor Heyerdahl the local people had made a groove in the volcanic rock.

The Mayor, who had led the Heyerdahl project, stood by as the von Daniken project proceeded, shaking his head and laughing. Von Daniken implies that this indicated that the statues could not be fashioned in this way, yet on the very next page he tells us of earlier "native" people who year after year had "hammered doggedly away at the unfinished models with their stone tools" (p. 131).

He actually acknowledges (on page 129) that "the stone tool theory may be valid for some of the small statues'' and here again his own writing shows his inconsistency, for he had already told us that the efforts of his own group left hardly a scratch on the rock. It seems their method of attack was wrong.

How Were the Statues Raised?

The second point of interest for Thor Heyerdahl was, "How were the statues raised?" and again the mayor had the answer. When asked why he had not told it before, his dignified reply was, "No one asked me" (p. 142). On the promise of $100 payment, he agreed to have one of the larger statues restored to its proper "home" on the temple wall.

With 11 other men he did just that, as the photographic evidence in *Aku-Aku* establishes. First, three large poles were used to lift the statue a fraction of an inch, and the mayor forced small stones underneath it. This process was repeated many times, with the stones getting larger all the time; the statue was roped into place to prevent it toppling over.

This statue was nearly ten feet wide across the shoulders, and weighed between 25 and 30 tons (p. 145). After one day only two poles were used, with five men on each. The mayor's youngest brother now became the "stone pusher," while the mayor himself became a sort of foreman, and actually beat the air in time as he encouraged them on, in his own language, "One, two, three! One, two three! Hold on, push under! Once more! One, two, three! One, two three!" (p. 146). Later in this chapter we shall see that von Daniken disparages the so-called "heave-ho" method concerning the pyramids of Egypt. These men on Easter Island certainly demonstrated how effective that "heave-ho" method can be.

The end of the operation is described very dramatically by Thor Heyerdahl. On the eighteenth day the two teams were working cautiously as they pulled on their ropes from opposite ends, one group on the beach and the other in the middle of the camp. All of a sudden the giant statue began to move perceptibly, and the order to halt was immediately given. On page 148 Heyerdahl tells how the giant statue was eventually in an upright position. At the crucial point many of the smaller stones and blocks tumbled down, but "the colossus only wobbled and came quietly to rest in an upright position." He goes on.

> The mystery of how the statues were raised had been resolved, and the stone "hat" on the statue could be raised in exactly the same way. The tower of stones could be taken away when both statue and cap were in position (p. 151).

Moving the Statues Across the Plain

Heyerdahl's third point was that the stone statues could be moved across the countryside of Easter Island. He arranged a great feast which was thoroughly enjoyed by the villagers. Then in something of a game 180 men took their places on a long rope that had been attached to the neck of one of the statues. At the first effort the rope broke, and the mayor was a little embarrassed; but he ordered the rope to be doubled and made fast again.

> Now the giant began to move — first in short jerks, but then suddenly it seemed to break loose .... the long lines of natives hauled patiently and yelled at the tops of their voices with enthusiasm. It moved as quickly as if they each were hauling an empty soap box (p. 150).

Then the statue was raised by the method above, and, like so many of its stone companions, it has become "a landmark visible far out to sea" (p. 193). It is a silent but convincing answer to Erich von

Daniken's hypothesis that "the 'heave-ho' method . . . . would have been impossible on Easter Island for lack of manpower" (p. 114 *Chariots*).

It is strange to notice the inconsistencies that appear so often in von Daniken's writings. We learn on pages 128-129 of *Return to the Stars* (later issued as *Gods from Outer Space*) that he "highly respects" Thor Heyerdahl, yet claims that "archaeologists all over the world" protested at his conclusions. Heyerdahl's was a "successful experiment," but it is von Daniken's conviction that Heyerdahl's method "can in no case be accepted for the excavation of the raw material for the colossal statues from the volcanic stone."

Let it simply be stated that I prefer to go along with the consistent and convincing arguments and practical demonstrations of Thor Heyerdahl. He has shown in passing how a von Daniken "chariot" has crashed, brought down in flames by some of those huge witnesses on Easter Island that seemed to bolster so impressively his way-out theories.

Nonsensical Talk About the Pyramids in Egypt

We have referred to the "heave-ho" method by which statues could be erected on Easter Island; von Daniken rejects this method as part of the answer to the way the stones of the Pyramids in Egypt were raised.

To illustrate the effectiveness of the method an incident which I personally observed is relevant.

Excavations were proceeding at Karnak, famous for so much recovered life from Egypt's past. I introduced myself to the French leader of the current excavations, but did not detain him, for it was obvious that he had much more to occupy his mind than to entertain a visitor from "down under." So I quietly wandered around, watching as huge stones, weighing about a ton each, were hauled up to resume the positions they had occupied long centuries before, back in those days when the Pharaoh's word was law in Egypt.

One group especially fascinated me — about 10 men, with a foreman supervising, were using a primitive pulley to lift those great stones. It was all done to music — perfect timing, with the new thrust taking place at just the right moment of the chant they were all singing.

This was a modern version of the "heave-ho" method, which von Daniken describes as the method suggested by "people with lively imaginations" (p. 114). I was watching a modern enactment of a scene that must have taken place day after day as the Pyramids were constructed.

Von Daniken writes caustically concerning the possibility that these "12-ton blocks were pushed skyward" by this "heave-ho" method (p. 101). It is more usual to estimate the weight of these stones as about 2½ tons each, approximately one-fifth the size von Daniken puts forward; though of course some were much larger than the 2½ tons average size.

Von Daniken puts forward the hypothesis that pyramids such as the Great Pyramid of Cheops were not the work of humans, but involved the activity of giants who came from beyond the earth.

Actually there are many pyramids, and the ruins of dozens of them can still be seen today stretching from Giza outside Cairo for many miles along the Nile.

According to the author of *Chariots of the Gods?*, one of the great problems in the building of these Pyramids was wood. He states that the Egyptians could not have imported it in sufficient quantity, for they did not have a large enough fleet (p. 97). Nor would they have made wooden rollers from their native trees, for the dates from the palms were urgently needed for food, and the trunks and fronds provided shelter for the dried-up land.

Since *Crash Go The Chariots* was originally published, a number of articles have appeared in various journals around the world, criticizing *Chariots of the Gods?* One of those articles is entitled "Chariots' Is Just So Much Humbug," in *Eternity* magazine dated January, 1974, written by Dr. Edward Yamauchi. Some of the points that follow are from that article. Dr. Yamauchi refers to the fact that Sneferu, the father of Cheops, with whose name the Great Pyramid is identified, actually sent a fleet of 40 ships to Phoenicia so that coniferous timber could be imported.

In any case, wood WAS used extensively for many purposes in ancient Egypt, as a visit to the Cairo Museum soon makes clear. Tutankhamen's treasures are but one indication of the large amount of wood that was used for furniture and other purposes. There are tomb paintings which include wooden sledges; such sledges would have been utilized in the construction of the pyramids, together with wooden scaffolding.

Wood was used extensively; one interesting reference, that of I.E.S. Edwards, tells of wooden baulks found *in situ* at Lisht. The fact is, while all the details of construction are not yet known, enough evidence is available from Egyptian reliefs to give the general picture. Rafts were used to float the limestone and granite blocks to within a few hundred yards of the Pyramids when the Nile was in flood. This was an annual event, though there were many times when poverty was rife because the Nile did NOT overflow.

How Long to Build a Pyramid?

Von Daniken's greatest criticism of traditionally held beliefs about the Pyramids relates to the time it would take to build them. He argues that several hundred thousand workmen would be required, and if they worked extraordinarily fast they could have completed the Great Pyramid of the Pharaoh Khufu in 664 years (p. 101). (Cheops and Khufu are the same Pharaoh.) The author of *Chariots of the Gods?* then implies that other hypotheses are totally unacceptable, and says:

> It seems obvious to me that the Pyramid cannot have been erected during a single lifetime.

This being the case, according to von Daniken, the Pharaoh Khufu conceivably forged the inscriptions that proclaimed his fame, and the Pyramid would have been erected "long before Khufu left his visiting card."

Who then really built the Great Pyramid? Von Daniken gives a "possible" answer: the Egyptian King Surid who rules in Egypt before the Flood (p. 102). Presumably this solves the problem of the hundreds of years required for the construction, since von Daniken has already referred to the Kings "before the Flood" who lived, according to the Sumerian King List, for hundreds of years. If this is how he solves the problem, it follows that he is accepting literally that these kings lived for so long, as he requires over 600 years for the erection of the Pyramid, and argues that this is not possible in the life of one king. Because he accepts that King Surid had the Pyramid built (p. 102), it follows that King Surid must have lived for over 600 years.

However, von Daniken also says that the Sumerian figures are "physically impossible" (p. 106). Presumably we must therefore not allow for the possibility of an Egyptian Pharaoh living for the great period of time that von Daniken needs for the building of the Pyramids.

In his "Critical Review" of *Chariots of the Gods?* my successor as Director of the Australian

Institute of Archaeology, Mr. Gordon Garner, provides valuable information at this point. Ahmed Fakhry (*The Pyramids*) and I.E.S. Edwards (*The Pyramids of Egypt*) are likewise relevant. Each shows a picture from the tomb of Djehutihotep, a 12th Dynasty nobleman. Edwards says:

> In this scene an alabaster statue of Djehutihotep, which probably weighed about 60 tons, is mounted on a sledge pulled by 172 men. Water or some other liquid is poured on the ground to lessen the friction and thus facilitate haulage (p. 266).

This colossus was over 6.5 meters high, and was on a wooden sledge that was dragged along by ropes.

Pharaohs' Names On Pyramids

The names of some of the Pharaohs are inscribed on blocks in various Pyramids (Edwards pp. 110ff, 205, 223, 238).

We have already stated that the Great Pyramid is only one of many stretching along the Nile, and one of these is the Pyramid of Meidum. Blocks have been located in this Pyramid with different dates at various points. Another Pyramid at Dahshur actually has a date on the northeastern corner stone — it was laid in the 21st year of Pharaoh Senefru. About half way up there is another date, this time dating to the same Pharaoh's 22nd year. If the dating is accurate, the maximum time elasped between the two dates would be under two years. This Pyramid is about two-thirds the size of the Great Pyramid, and even if the dates given are not accurate — perhaps the boastful exaggeration of the Pharaoh's builders — it is clear that nothing like the 664 years demanded by von Daniken is required.

The ancient historian Herodotus says it took four separate groups of 100,000 men 20 years (each group working for three months of the year) to build the actual Pyramid. An extra 10 years was said to be taken for building a causeway: the stone had to be hauled across this after being transported from its landing point at the Nile nearby. Work on the substructures went on at the same time.

I have said that the Pyramid stones averaged about 2½ tons each, and I have also referred to the fact that 172 workmen were able to drag a 60-ton colossus on a wooden sledge. Eight men could handle one stone block of the average size of the Pyramid stones, and if I were to accept Herodotus' figures as being approximately correct, a simple mathematical calculation shows that nothing like 600 years was required for the construction of the Great Pyramid. If 100,000 men worked three months each year, they would have moved 115,000 blocks. As Cheops reigned for 23 years (Edwards, p. 282), the erection of this Pyramid in his reign is entirely conceivable.

How well I remember those huge blocks that I saw being recovered and restored at Karnak, by a comparatively small group of modern Egyptian workmen. The "heave-ho" technique, utilizing ropes and pulleys, which was used in ancient times (and which is also used today), is a method despised by von Daniken.

Other relevant points from Edward Yamauchi's article, referred to above, also make interesting reading. Von Daniken says that it would have been more practical to locate the building site nearer the eastern quarries in order to shorten transport distances. Yamauchi gives the answer that not only Cheops' Pyramid, but also the other eighty (approximately) Pyramids and burial sites were located on the west bank of the Nile "because the Egyptians viewed the setting of the sun in the west as the land of the dead."

Von Daniken also makes the point that the precise fitting of the stones as well as their number and weight must be attributed to super-human efforts, but the answer is that despite the admirable nature of the construction of the Pyramids, it is hardly super-human. The art of working in very hard stone was known to the Egyptians before the time of the Pyramids. As early as the First Dynasty (3,100 B.C.), the ancient Egyptians utilized copper saws which could cut through any kind of limestone, the type of stone predominant in the Giza Pyramid.

Calculations From the Great Pyramid

In the earlier version of *Crash Go The Chariots*, we discussed von Daniken's calculations for "pi." Since that time, von Daniken has stated (in a radio debate with this author) that there is a mistake in the English edition of *Chariots of the Gods?* on this point, resulting from a mistranslation of the original German. Therefore, we do not repeat the calculations we gave relating to "pi."

However, von Daniken makes much of the figures associated with the measurements of the Pyramids (page 99), and correspondence from around the world since the first edition of *Crash Go The Chariots* appeared indicates that there is great interest in this aspect of the Pyramids; the following brief outline is relevant.

From the time that Napoleon conquered Egypt, remarkable measurements associated with the Pyramids have been known. His engineers found that the east side of the Great Pyramid at Gizeh pointed due east, and that it was directly aligned to the polar axis of the earth.

Since that time a movement centering around "Pyramidology" has developed, with this Great Pyramid painstakingly measured by experts from many fields — archaeologists, astronomers, cartographers, and others — some of whom have then offered their highly controversial interpretations that depend on the Pyramid's measurements.

One of the most famous "experts" was the Scottish astronomer, Charles Piazzi Smith, who made special instruments and spent several months measuring the Pyramid and its environs. Among other figures he stated that there were 36,524 "Pyramid inches" around the square at its base and suggested that this was almost exactly 100 times the number of days in a year. However, this is interesting only when we accept his fundamental assumption as to what a "Pyramid inch" is. This measurement was his own creation, and it does not take much thought to realize that wonderful results can be "established" if we can first set our own standards of measurement.

Smith and his colleagues also argued that the empty stone sarcophagus that had originally been found in the King's chamber of the Pyramid represented a standard of measurement which was actually the ancestor of the British system of volume. That empty coffin would have held about 1¼ tons of water. To base a theory about modern standards of measurement on an ancient coffin that had been shut up for many centuries inside a huge artificial mountain is simply ludicrous.

Various religious groups became interested in the Pyramid measurements, and the great Egyptologist, W.M. Flinders Petrie, was at first taken in by Smith's theories, mainly because his own father had adopted them. However, Petrie went to Egypt and showed that in fact Smith's measurements were inaccurate, despite his expensive instruments that had been constructed especially for this project. Petrie disproved the whole basis of Pyramidology, but the theories have persisted to this day, in spite of the fact that prophecies, based on the Pyramid's measurements, have not come to pass. They included a Great War that was supposed to break out in 1928, the return of Christ to earth in 1936, and the end of the world in 1953.

I stress that the construction of the Pyramid, including its measurements, is amazingly complex. No one having once studied the facts would state otherwise. However, the theories that von Daniken and others touch on are quite unacceptable when the facts are studied objectively. Sprague and Catherine de Camp point out that if one has enough figures to juggle, remarkable results can be achieved from unlikely material. They can state:

> Borchardt, as an anti-Pyramidological joke, derived a base e of natural logarithms from the slope of Sahura's Pyramid. Barnard, by juggling the dimensions of the Temple of Artmis at Ephesus, got the moon's diameter, the length of the lunar months, and the date of the building.

When one considers such facts, it is somewhat pathetic to put another von Daniken statement alongside this quotation. He asked:

> Yet who is so ingenuous as to believe that the Pyramid was nothing but the tomb of a king? From now on who will consider the transmission of mathematics, astronomical signs as pure chance?

As for his question concerning its being "nothing but the tomb of a king," the very fact that an empty sarcophagus was found suggests that one purpose of the Pyramid was that it would be a tomb. It is a fact that most of the Pyramids were designed as tombs for Pharaohs and royal personages. I have already pointed out that they were located on the west bank of the Nile because the Egyptians related the setting of the sun in the west to the land of the dead. Approximately 45 mummified bodies have been recovered from the known Pyramids, and the opinion of archaeologists, that these massive edifices were constructed as tombs and memorials for the Pharaoh then ruling, is still widely accepted despite the views of Erich von Daniken.

Surely, yet another "chariot" has crashed, this time into the base of the Great Pyramid of the Pharaoh Khufu, or Cheops, as the Greeks called him.

Strange Talk About Embalming

Before we leave Egypt, let us consider yet another peculiar von Daniken hypothesis, this time about embalming. Once again, a personal episode is of some relevance.

During a visit to Cairo, my host was the Director of the Cairo Museum. He spoke English fluently. Our conversation ranged over many aspects of archaeology, not the least of which is the near-embarrassment Egypt suffers at having such huge quantities of artifacts recovered from ancient Egyptian sites. This is obvious to even the casual visitor who sees a huge statue of Rameses 11 in the mud alongside the formerly sacred pool (now a stagnant waterhole) at Memphis, as well as those magnificent Colossae of Memnon which now stand in a farmer's field, unattended except by his silent crops.

I assured the Director I did not want a personally conducted tour of the Museum, for there was so much I wanted to see and to photograph for myself: the Stela of Pharaoh Merneptah, with its first historic reference to Israel as a nation; the famous Tutankhamen tomb findings; the mummies of Egyptian Pharaohs; and many more such recovered treasures. So I was given a free pass, and had a most enjoyable morning wandering around, photographing, questioning, making notes — and not the least of my enjoyments was my time spent in the "mummy room," which brings me to the point of this story.

I presented my pass at the door, only to be told that I still must pay. I insisted that I had a free pass — there it was, in perfectly good Egyptian script. However, the attendant was determined, and insisted that I must pay. I asked him to bring me to the Supervisor, for I was sure that I was not meant to pay. However, the Supervisor looked at my pass and then sided with the attendant. He insisted, "You must pay to get into the mummy room."

"No," I said, equally determined by now. "Here is my ticket signed by your Director. I am to have free admission to the Museum."

The Supervisor looked at the ticket again, then his eyes lit up.

"You must pay," he said, slamming the ticket down in triumph. "This is only for admission to the Museum, and there is a special charge for admission to the mummy room." I saw the funny side of the incident and paid up the nominal extra charge. The Supervisor, the attendant, and I were now very good friends!

Wizened Old Pharaohs

In a way, the mummy room proved to be something of a disappointment. I looked at the famous Seti I — one of Egypt's cruelest rulers, though a renowned military campaigner. There in a glass case was his actual head — like a wizened old, old man; his jugular vein protruded in a most gruesome way. That seemed to be the picture right around the room, with Pharaoh after Pharaoh merely a gruesome object in a glass case.

Erich von Daniken has his own hypothesis on the subject of embalming. He asks:

Or did some gods (space travellers) transmit their knowledge of how corpses can be reawakened after a special treatment to a quick-witted prince of royal blood? . . . .

The high priests, who actually did possess some knowledge of such reawakenings, did a great deal to encourage this cult, for their class did good business out of it . . . . Are we perhaps getting a clue to the incredible age of the men named in the texts if we assume that they were mummified or frozen? (pp. 106-7).

Much more follows, and it becomes clear that the author of *Chariots* is putting forward the theory that mummification is in the same category as modern ideas of deep-freezing bodies for "re-awakening" hundreds, or even thousands, of years later when medical techniques have been perfected. He talks about frozen blood, preserved human bones, deep-freeze cemeteries — and embalming.

However, this association is quite unjustified by the facts. While not advocating that there is the possibility of frozen bodies being thawed out when medical advance ensures greater longevity of life, it should be recognized that those new ideas are quite different from the processes involved in the Egyptian practice of embalming.

There is clear evidence that the extraordinarily dry climate of Egypt encouraged the Egyptians to preserve their dead even in pre-historic times, and as time went by, religious practices became involved with the process itself.

The four sons of the god Horus were supposed to sit on the tops of four funerary jars, and in those jars were placed various internal organs of the deceased person. Even the heart was removed. I have seen inscriptions in the Valley of the Kings showing a man's heart supposedly being weighed against the feather of truth.

Regardless of the argument of Erich van Daniken as to embalming and re-awakenings in this life, this was NOT the Egyptian hope. Rather, they were to pronounce certain magic formulas in the life beyond the grave, so that their inward parts would return to their bodies, and a new life would commence. They thought of this as having some continuum with the present life, for man conceives of himself as eternal when blessed of the gods; and man's body is part of himself. In some way that the Egyptians could not understand or explain, the body would be involved in the future life. For this reason, token amounts of food were placed in the tombs, together with wooden or other forms of ushabti (servants), and various implements that spoke of the continuation of life. Nevertheless, it was recognized that even a Pharaoh could not provide enough food for an eternal lifetime. The amounts in the tombs were then only a token provision.

Strangely, the Egyptians do not seem to have preserved the brain, this only being removed before embalming took place. What sort of a future earthly life could be promised to a man who was revived without a brain? The possibility is of course absurd, despite von Daniken's hypothesis.

As I have said, the dry climate itself was a factor in the preservation of bodies, and some bodies have been recovered that were preserved though not embalmed.

Man Is Distinctive In Three Ways

It is relevant to state that the Egyptians DID have some idea of immortality, and perhaps there is an answer to this question, or at least some light can be shed on its source.

The archaeological evidence indicates that man is distinct from all other creatures in at least three separate ways. These are: a knowledge of God, a belief in life beyond the grave, and the ability to communicate by spoken words. These are distinctively human abilities, and their virtual universal presence is borne out by archaeological research.

Man has an inherent knowledge that there is a power beyond himself and, in site after site, we find images of gods and altars. But no bird, no animal, ever made such an image or built an altar to a god. This fits the Bible statement that man is made in the image of God — of God Who is infinite, of God Who is eternal. Man has a strange understanding of his own potential, his own share in the nature of the eternal God. He seeks for that God or gods, and believes that he himself will somehow live forever in the presence of God or gods.

The ancient Egyptians who practiced embalming, and left food and implements in their graves, were simply demonstrating that they were linked to a long line of peoples across the face of the globe having such beliefs.

3

THAT SURPRISING CLAIM
ABOUT THE ELECTRIFIED ARK

(The dialogue in this chapter has been slightly expanded, since the first edition, by further conversation with Jeff Peers.)

Von Daniken collates many facts from many areas — areas of learning as well as geographic areas. However, his writing is ludicrous at times, with pathetically weak statements that surely cannot be taken seriously. One of the weakest examples is what he has to say about the Ark of the Covenant.

The Ark of the Covenant was a chest in which Moses was to place certain sacred objects, all of which had spiritual significance. Precise instructions were given as to the size and covering of this very special box. When the Israelites were on the march it was to be carried only by divinely appointed persons, and it was to be treated as a holy object; for it spoke by symbols of the Being of God. Jews and Christians see very clear spiritual significance in all this, for the objects placed inside were of spiritual and historical significance — the tablets of the law, a pot of manna from the wilderness, and Aaron's rod that budded, which symbolically spoke of newness of life with God.

An incident is recorded in II Samuel, Chapter 6, of a man named Uzzah grabbing the Ark and being struck dead, at the time when King David was moving the Ark toward Jerusalem. Uzzah paid the price for sacrilege.

"Undoubtedly the Ark Was Electrically Charged!"

Von Daniken apparently does not doubt the fact of the incident, but this is how he explains it:

> When passing cattle shook and threatened to overturn the Ark, Uzzah grabbed hold of it. He fell dead on the spot, as if struck by lightning. Undoubtedly the Ark was electrically charged! (p. 59).

Unfortunately this is typical of the approach in *Chariots*. A fact of history is taken, it is recognized that there is an apparent difficulty in explaining it, so a way-out theory is put forward as the one possible solution. In this case, the sacred Ark of the Covenant was electrically charged! Nonsense.

I am not an electrical expert, so I called my friend Jeff Peers who is involved in electronics. He took time to check his facts, then called me back. What he had to say confirmed my own thinking.

The conversation went something like this:

WILSON: Jeff, what about von Daniken's claim that the Ark of the Covenant must have been electrically charged when Uzzah was struck dead for touching it? Without being too technical, would it be possible for the Ark to have been electrically charged?

PEERS: I've now discussed this theory with some of my colleagues, and there are a number of things that ought to be said.

WILSON: Right. Let's start with von Daniken's claim that a condenser was formed by the gold plates, one being positive and the other negative.

PEERS: If we take a cubit as being 18 inches, the Ark was a box about 3'9" x 2'3" x 2'3". The instructions given to Moses are very clear — the wood of the box was to be completely overlaid with gold. The rings on the corners were also to be overlaid with gold, and so were the staves with which the Ark was to be carried.

WILSON: Are you saying that there was virtually only ONE metal plate, and so there was no possibility of there being one negative and one positive?

PEERS: Yes — if it was charged, any one part would be in fact part of the rest, and the conditions needed for a condenser are simply not fulfilled. There would automatically be a short circuit.

WILSON: What are the requirements for a condenser?

PEERS: There must be two pieces that are separated by an insulator. Theoretically it is possible for there to be only one piece of metal, but it would need to have an insulator in the middle — for example, a piece of wood — so that for the purposes of the condenser, the metal was acted upon as though it were two pieces of metal, separated by the wood. The technical name for the insulating piece of wood is the dielectric.

WILSON: I gather all this was not possible with the Ark because it was completely overlaid with gold. There was no insulator to make possible a negative and a positive plate?

PEERS: That's right. And what's more, over the top of the Ark the Mercy Seat was placed, and it was made of pure gold. It was exactly the same length and breadth as the Ark, and so it fitted completely over the top. Even if von Daniken argued that somehow there was a space inside (which is not so according to the Bible), that space would have been completely covered by the Mercy Seat on the top.

WILSON: So no one could put his hand inside to make contact with the supposed two plates?

PEERS: Exactly — so even if we accepted von Daniken's hypothesis — despite the fact that it opposes the instructions given to Moses — there would still not be a condenser.

WILSON: So when Uzzah touched the Ark he was not killed by an electric charge given out from a condenser?

PEERS: Wait, that's not all. A condenser must be charged, and a perfectly legitimate question to ask is: "Where did the electricity come from to charge a condenser?" The condenser is simply a storage place of electricity. Where did Moses plug in for power in the first place?

Static Electricity?

WILSON: Excuse the silly question, but what about static electricity? Sometimes you can get a small charge when you get out of an automobile, when you move away from the insulation of the rubber tires and so on.

PEERS: It's not a silly question, but it still could not explain Uzzah's death. A comparable situation to the car would be for the whole Ark to become one "plate" and for the earth itself to become the other — the insulator between them would be the air gap. But the greater the air gap the smaller the electric charge, and even in a car you don't get anything like a fatal shock — usually only a few volts. To get a fatal shock you need enough volts and enough amperage as well. When you touch the spark on a motor engine you can be in contact with as much as 15,000 volts, but it is not fatal because the amperage is not there. On the other hand, you will still not be killed when you put your fingers across the terminal

45

of a car battery, for though there might be 100 amps there is only 12 volts — you must have both the amperage and the volts for the shock to be effective enough to kill a man.

WILSON: I gather you reject this whole idea of static electricity with the Ark. However, even if you DID concede this point, what would be the likelihood of static build-up to a fatal level?

PEERS: In this case, if it be insisted that there was a static build-up (which I stress I cannot concede), it would be so minor as to be irrelevant.

Any such hypothetical static build-up in the Ark would be only minor compared with the build-up in an automobile. Furthermore every time the priests rested — as they would on a long journey — and lowered the Ark to the ground, there would be an immediate static discharge. Therefore the only static charge that could build up would be while the Ark was in the carrying position. Even so, the charge would not build up because there would be a constant discharge, however minor, through the carrying poles and the priests to the earth. This hypothetical static voltage could not build up to a high level since, as we have noted, they would hardly carry the Ark for long distances without resting.

Why Would Only One Man Be Killed?

WILSON: If Uzzah was killed by an electric charge, surely it would have also killed the priests?

PEERS: That's another point. I've made a careful search of the Bible references and there is nothing said about the priests having protective clothes or special shoes. If a man such as Uzzah, in contact with the supposed "earth plate," could be killed by "joining" the plates — that is, the earth and the Ark, it stands to reason that the priests also would be killed every time they touched the ground or touched anyone or anything in contact with the ground. They carried the Ark at times, as when they placed it in this cart, and then later when they transferred it to a man's house.

WILSON: So if von Daniken's hypothesis was correct, the priests also must have been killed?

PEERS: That's right. Even their carrying poles were completely covered with gold, so they were automatically in contact with what von Daniken is referring to as the metal plates.

WILSON: Von Daniken is of course making a case that Moses was given very specific instructions because of the special nature of this object as a means of communication. Have you any comment?

PEERS: I've been studying that too. The fact is that God gave very specific instructions for ALL that was associated with this Tabernacle which was to symbolize His presence in the midst of His people. Everyday things like dishes and spoons were included, but von Daniken makes nothing of that at all. He has missed the whole point of the instructions, for as these things were set apart they were reminding the Israelites that spiritual values touched all departments of life. This was not just a magical formula, or a new revelation of science as to electric power.

WILSON: So you don't think Uzzah died of an electric shock?

PEERS: There is no mention of it in the Bible. Von Daniken says he died "as if struck by lightning. Undoubtedly the Ark was electrically charged!" There simply is no basis for this claim; it is nothing but an unwarranted assumption. In fact, if we go over to Numbers, Chapter 4, verse 15, we find that the warning is given that if someone touched ANY of the holy things, that person would die. The same sort of warning was given when Moses was receiving the Law on Mount Sinai — the Israelites did not dare to approach that mountain.

The Cherubim As a Microphone

WILSON: Let's move on to von Daniken's claim that one of the cherubim figures above the Ark could have been used as a microphone. Have you a comment?

PEERS: The Bible makes it clear that this simply was not the case. In Exodus 25:22, it states that God would commune with Moses from BETWEEN the cherubim ABOVE the Mercy Seat. Von Daniken states that God would "speak to him from the mercy seat" and then suggests that "one of the two cherubim on the mercy seat acted as a magnet, the loudspeaker. . . ." Both statements are on page 58 of his book. The verse I've just quoted makes it clear that von Daniken is wrong in both his assumptions, provided we take the Bible literally, as von Daniken himself is doing at this point.

WILSON: What about this whole idea of a magnet and a loudspeaker — would it technically be possible in association with the Ark?

PEERS: This would have to be a condenser microphone of course. In such a microphone the two plates would move in and out from a dielectric — that is, an insulating strip between two plates. It's only a fractional movement, and the voltage varies according to the distance moved — the further the plates are apart, the lower the voltage. A microphone works on vibrations moving the parts that make it up, thus producing varying charges of electricity — as when the diaphragm of a telephone pulls up and down as a conversation proceeds. This causes an electric current which is then amplified, and so on,

WILSON: Are you saying the cherubim COULD have been used as von Daniken suggests?

PEERS: No. Technically the Ark as described in the Bible could not be made in such a way that it would act as a microphone or speaker. In any case it would not be possible physically, even if the instructions to Moses were changed and a condenser was made. The amount of voltage produced by such a condenser would register at something like 10 to the minus 6 — only millionths of one volt. It would be quite impossible to use it to send out the volume of noise required to communicate with a space ship, as von Daniken suggests at page 58. The whole thing is ludicrous.

WILSON: Could we use it, as von Daniken suggests, now that we have our modern scientific knowledge?

PEERS: No. The voltage level would be much too low, and you need other electronic gear besides a condenser to make contact. Even the essential coils of wire are not referred to in the precise instructions given to Moses. This particular aspect was not discovered until 1819 by a man named Ersted — over 3,000 years after the time of Moses. He showed the relationship between magnetism and electricity.

WILSON: You mentioned "magnetism" — von Daniken refers to a magnet in this context. Have you a comment?

PEERS: The use of the magnet was not known until the time of the Greeks, many hundreds of years after Moses. They called it a lode stone. In the days of Moses, there was no knowledge of the fact that vibrations could cause electricity, let alone the ability to implement all the complexities involved in verbal communication with a space ship.

Our conversation continued for some time, as my friend explained technical points. If I had not been convinced before, I certainly was then. Von Daniken's hypothesis simply does not stand serious investigation.

"Without Actually Consulting Exodus ...."

This "electrically charged" criticism does not end there. In the same paragraph in which he says,

"Undoubtedly the Ark was electrically charged!" von Daniken also says:

> Without actually consulting Exodus, I seem to remember that the Ark was often surrounded by flashing sparks and that Moses made use of this 'transmitter' whenever he needed help and advice (pp. 58-59).

Is this meant to be taken as evidence of serious research? In his own words we find that he puts forward part of his way-out theory "without actually consulting Exodus." There are far too many Bible critics who know all about the Bible, tell you it is full of mistakes and so on, but cannot put their finger on one when they are handed a Bible. Von Daniken makes his case even weaker when he goes on to say, "I seem to remember." How strange it is to rely on such a vague approach when he is presenting a view which will be disturbing to thousands of Christians and Jews as they read!

"I seem to remember." "Without actually consulting Exodus." The pity is that he did NOT consult Exodus, for in fact his memory has let him down. There is no reference in Exodus — or anywhere else in Scripture — to the Ark's being "surrounded by flashing sparks."

That is not all. There are a number of occasions recorded in the Book of Exodus where God spoke to Moses BEFORE the Ark was constructed. Exodus chapter 6 records one of a number of such occasions. What was the "transmitter" used on those earlier occasions before the Ark was constructed? The Bible certainly does not support the ideas of Erich von Daniken at this point.

Sadly, the "Chariots of the Gods" have been short-circuited again. They crash in searing flames when confronted by the evidence from an old Book which a Psalmist once referred to as a light — "A light unto my path." One of the New Testament writers commented that that same "Word of God" is full of power — "The Word of God is quick and powerful" (Hebrews 4:12). It has been called "That Impregnable Rock of Holy Scripture." Through the centuries it has been well able to defend itself. It will continue to do so, despite the wild theories of Erich von Daniken and the question he asks on the cover of his book, "Was God an Astronaut?"

4

OUTFLOODING THE FLOOD

Yet another of Erich von Daniken's strange views relates to the story of the great Flood which is recorded in the Bible. Some scholars raise such questions as whether it was "local" (confined to the Fertile Crescent) or "universal" (world-wide), but Erich von Daniken "outfloods" them all. He has the original version coming from South America! This is his viewpoint of the famous *Epic of Gilgamesh*, in which the flood story is told.

Archaeologically, it can be shown that the author has put forward an argument that must be dismissed by fact. Perhaps it should first be stated that this Epic contains the Babylonian story of the Flood, a record that was copies by the Assyrians at a much later time.

"Parallel To Genesis"

Von Daniken makes the claim that "the main thread of the Epic of Gilgamesh runs parallel to the

Biblical Book of Genesis'' (p. 64), but in fact, the similarity of this Epic to the Bible record is limited to the Flood story. The Babylonian Creation story is known as *Enuma Elish* (from the first words, meaning "When from above . . .") while a more recently translated Epic — the Epic of Atrahasis — brings together parts of the other two Epics. However, none of them pre-date the Biblical record. The scriptural account is now recognized as the oldest of all these records, and certainly it is not copied from the Babylonian version.

Von Daniken contends the Bible account is a second-hand one (p. 68), but the evidence is against such an argument. As Professor W.F. Albright points out in *Yahweh and the Gods of Canaan*, the Bible record contains archaic features dating it before any Mesopotamian version that is "preserved in cuneiform sources" (p. 86). Those "cuneiform sources" include the Epic of Gilgamesh and the Epic of Atrahasis.

The Bible account is not the second-hand one. Rather, the Babylonian and Assyrian versions are later distortions, with many differences from the Biblical record. The superiority of the Bible version is established.

To substantiate such a statement, let us look at the facts. First, we need briefly to summarize the Epic of Gilgamesh as it relates to the Flood.

What the Epic Is All About

Utnapishtim was the Babylonian Noah; with his boatman, Pazu-Amurri, he went through seven days of terrible flood. A very good friend of Gilgamesh named Enkidu had died at the decree of the gods, and Gilgamesh realized that he too must eventually die. He heard of Utnapishtim, who had escaped death, and he set out to find him so that he could learn from him the secret of immortality.

Gilgamesh eventually found Utnapishtim, the only man who had ever obtained everlasting life. Gilgamesh asked Utnapishtim how he had found this secret. Utnapishtim then told how one of the gods urged him to destroy his house and build a vessel. Utnapishtim obeyed the voice of the gods, built a great boat, and eventually the expected flood came.

Gods Cowering Like Dogs

Before long the gods themselves were terrified, and we read:

Even the gods were afeared at the deluge, took to flight and went up to the heaven of Anu, cowered they like dogs and crouched down at the outer defenses.

This certainly is a very different concept of God from that given in the Bible record of the flood. We surely could not think of the God of the Bible cowering like a dog or being terrified by a deluge.

Another translation of the Epic tells of the goddess Ishtar in great distress:

Ishtar cried like a woman in travail, wailed the queen of the gods with her beautiful voice: "Those creatures are turned to clay, since I commanded evil in the assembly of the gods; because I commanded evil in the assembly of the gods, for the destruction of my people I commanded battle. I alone bore my people; like spawn of fishes they fill the sea." The gods along with the Anunnaki wept with her, the gods bowed, sat as they wept; closed were their lips; (silent their) assembly.

The crude polytheism of this Babylonian Epic is obviously vastly different from the majestic, yet simple, Bible record.

When the flood was all over and Utnapishtim came out, he made an offering to the gods, and the Epic of Gilgamesh tells us:

And the gods smelled the savour, the gods smelled the sweet savour, the gods gathered like flies about the priest of the offering.

These poor gods had not been fed — because mankind had been destroyed — and so they gathered like flies as soon as Utnapishtim remembered their need and did something about it! The God Who is revealed in the Bible does not need the offerings of a man to sate His hunger, nor could we ever imagine its being said of the true God of the Heavens that He has come like flies to an offering.

After that, the gods were angry amongst themselves, and began to blame each other for their foolishness in bringing this flood on man. It is all very different from the Bible picture of God waiting patiently for 120 years while a Gospel of mercy was preached. The true God acted in judgment only when man continued to reject His ways.

Similarities — and Differences

Other writers besides von Daniken have pointed out similarities to the Bible story: in each record there is supposedly a final revelation to the hero of the flood, warning him that a deluge is coming which is unknown to everyone else. However, in the Bible story, Noah is told to warn others so that they too can accept the way of salvation if they so desire.

In each case the hero builds a vessel which is lined within and without with pitch. The Bible and other versions describe the flood in which all others are destroyed, and tell of the great ship resting on a mountain, and of certain birds that were sent out. Each record tells how the hero disembarks and offers a sacrifice, and then says that such a deluge shall not be visited on man again.

However, the dissimilarities are even more important than the similarities, and they clearly point to the fact that the Babylonian version is a corruption of the Biblical original.

As we have seen, the Bible account is very different from the Babylonian legend. The gross polytheism of the Babylonian story — with gods crouching in fear, and then swarming like hungry flies to a sacrifice — is quite alien to the noble concept of the almighty God presented in the Bible record.

As we compare the Babylonian and other ancient records of the Flood with the Bible record, it becomes clear that the Bible record is infinitely superior. It does not bear the marks of the grotesque, the superstititious, or the magical. Its description is picturesque, but it is truly acceptable to the man or the woman prepared to accede to the great concept of a God Who can and does reveal Himself.

Did the Epic of Gilgamesh Come From
South America?

The above material is relevant also as background to the Epic of Gilgamesh, for this is another topic on which von Daniken has his own hypothesis. He suggests that the descendants of Gilgamesh might have brought the Epic with them from South America, thus explaining why similarities exist between the two cultures that are otherwise unexplained. For good measure, he even suggests the possibility that the Epic found its way into the library rooms of the Egyptian court where Moses would have had access to it. Von Daniken then summarizes:

> If we work on the hypothesis that the Epic of Gilgamesh came to Egypt from the Sumerians by way of the Assyrians and Babylonians, and that the young Moses found it there and adapted it for his own ends, then the Sumerian story of the Flood, and not the biblical one, would be the genuine account (p. 69).

The logic is hard to follow, but three points should be noticed. First, we have already seen that scholars accept that the Biblical account includes archaisms that indicate that it preceded the Babylonian and Assyrian versions of the Flood.

Secondly, a fragment of the Epic has been found at the ancient Biblical city of Megiddo in Israel, and this pre-dated the copy from the palace of the Assyrian King Ashurbanipal by many hundreds of years. This was before the time of Moses, but not before Abraham.

A far more realistic reconstruction, one that would not distort known evidence, is that just as this Epic of Gilgamesh was carried across the Fertile Crescent from Mesopotamia to Palestine, so could a similar journey be true as told in the early chapters of Genesis. Perhaps Abraham, the friend of God, brought them across that same tract of territory when he migrated from Ur to the land of Canaan. In that way they could eventually come into the hands of Moses, having been brought into Egypt by the descendants of Abraham and Jacob.

Thirdly, flood traditions are known world-wide and are often remarkably close to the Bible record. Robert T. Boyd has this telling summary:

> Is the Bible account of the great flood the only record known? There are no less than thirty-three separate racial records among people and races who are living today. Of this number, only the Egyptian and Scandinavian records fail to coincide absolutely with Moses' account. They differ in that their records attribute partial destruction to water and the rest by "direct acts" of many gods. Greek tradition mentions a warning from gods that a great flood would be brought upon the earth because of man's wickedness, that an ark was built, that it rested on a high mountain, and

that a dove was sent out twice. "Faha," whom the Chinese say is their founder, is represented as having escaped with his wife, three sons, and three daughters from a flood that was sent "because man rebelled against heaven." The English, Hindus, Aztecs of Mexico, Incas of Peru, the Fiji Islanders, and even the American Indians have traditional stories about a flood. (in *Tells, Tombs and Treasure*, p. 72).

We have seen that Erich von Daniken suggests that the Epic could have originated in South America — from the Tiahuanaco region (p. 69) — and we have referred to the fragment found at Megiddo. Writing is known in Peru only from about 500 A.D., though their culture was there about a thousand years earlier. Even if they had immediately put their records into writing at that earlier date, it would still be about a thousand years after the Epic of Gilgamesh was being carried across the Fertile Crescent to find its way to Megiddo, where it remained until its excavation in this generation.

To suggest that the Epic of Gilgamesh — the Babylonian story of the Flood — could have had its origin in South America, then to find its way into an Egyptian court where Moses would have had access to it, is absurd. It was known long before the establishment of the South American settlements to which von Daniken refers.

The Book of Exodus From Gilgamesh

Much more can be said about von Daniken's theories and interpretations relating to the Epic of Gilgamesh, but one other aspect is very relevant for the Bible student. We have already seen that he suggests that the main thread of Gilgamesh runs parallel to Genesis; mention must also be made of a statement, even harder to credit, found on page 59 of *Chariots of the Gods?*:

> Or does the whole account in Exodus come from the Epic of Gilgamesh? Even that is possible.

Such a statement is virtually incredible. In the first chapter of Exodus, we learn of the birth of Moses, and the Book itself is a historical record of Israel as it became a nation. It certainly could NOT have come from the Babylonian Epic of Gilgamesh!

The Chariots Crash In the Mounds Of Antiquity

We have seen that the Babylonian Epic of Gilgamesh touches on the story of the Flood, and that von Daniken makes another blunder regarding the list on which the names of ten kings who lived "before the flood" are recorded. He lists the total reigns as coming to 456,000 years, then says:

> Periods of years that are quite incomprehensible to our way of thinking, although the names of all the rulers exist in long lists, neatly perpetuated on seals and coins (p. 41).

This is the "Sumerian King List". We will not argue as to the figure of 456,000, though in checking two different sources we find the figure is 432,000. What we do challenge is that the names of these kings are "neatly perpetuated on seals and coins." The original list was actually eight kings — the Babylonian priest Berossos expanded it to ten. In 1923 an almost complete translation of the Sumerian original was published. However, it certainly did not come from "seals and coins", but from clay tablets. Cylinder seals were utilized by kings and others, with symbols associated with their own authority, but it was on clay tablets, not seals, that Sumerian records were kept. Coins were not minted until about 600 B.C. — making von Daniken off 2,000 years or more in his calculations.

Incidentally, this is further evidence that von Daniken's suggestion that the Epic came to Sumer from South America is totally unacceptable. The dating is simply much earlier than the time von Daniken is considering.

In any case, von Daniken has the Ark landing on Mt. Ararat in modern Turkey (which by the way differs from the Epic of Gilgamesh — Mt. Ararat is the Biblical site, with Mount Nisir claimed in the Gilgamesh Epic). For his theory to be seriously considered, surely the Ark would have landed in South America. This is yet another apparent contradiction.

More could be said about von Daniken's hypothesis relating to the Epic of Gilgamesh, but our point is made. Another chariot has crashed into the mound of ancient Megiddo where that early fragment of the Epic of Gilgamesh was found.

It is interesting to realize that Megiddo is the site of the Biblical Armageddon, for "Har Megiddo" is "Mount Megiddo." Von Daniken is not the first, nor will he be the last, who has foundered when he has presumed to attack what has been called that impregnable Rock of Holy Scripture.

5

THAT "ATOMIC EXPLOSION" AT SODOM

One of the strange things about *Chariots of the Gods?* is that von Daniken accepts various writers and theories as authoritative when it suits him, but rejects them if they happen not to be in line with his present point of view.

This applies to his use of the Bible, as well as to other books. A good example is found on page 52 of the second Australian edition, from which the quotations in this book are taken. There von Daniken refers to the giants that are mentioned in Genesis, chapter 6, At that point he appears to be accepting the Bible as an authoritative source book; but then he goes on to discuss the events relating to the destruction of the cities of Sodom and Gomorrah as told in Genesis 19:1-28. Now von Daniken offers his own way-out hypothesis on the Biblical text, adding to the story in a way that is quite unjustified.

To understand our criticisms, it is necessary to

show that this story is a factual record and can be accepted by scientists and Christian scholars who approach the record objectively.

I have the privilege of being Consulting Editor to *Bible and Spade*, a quarterly digest of Biblical Archaeology published by Word of Truth Productions, (P.O. Box 2, Burnt Hills, New York, 12027).

A recent issue has an elaborate article entitled "Have Sodom and Gomorrah Been Found?" by my colleague, Bryant Wood, M.A., M.Sc. With his approval the following summary and comments are now included. They give an effective answer to Erich von Daniken's unfounded claims as to a supposed nuclear blast at Sodom.

Investigations That Commenced Fifty Years Ago

In 1924 Professor W.F. Albright and the Reverend M. Kyle investigated the areas surrounding the southern end of the Dead Sea, and they concluded that the five Biblical "Cities of the Plain" lay buried beneath this relatively shallow body of water. The northern half is much deeper — the southern portion is of relatively recent origin. Many scholars have accepted that the "Vale of Siddim" (Genesis 14:3) is buried beneath this southern section, especially as that verse has an editorial comment concerning the valley — "which is the Salt Sea" (this point at Genesis 14:3 indicates that the valley had become a sea).

Albright found no cities dating to Abraham's time in the immediate vicinity, and he concluded that the Cities of the Plain (including Sodom and Gomorrah) therefore were buried beneath the Dead Sea.

Albright and Kyle located a site known as Bab edh-Dhra in the nearby Moabite foothills, and theorized that this was a high place, regularly visited by the residents of Sodom, Gomorrah, and the other Cities of the Plain. They believed that when the cities were destroyed, the high place was deserted for some centuries.

This reconstruction was widely accepted by scholars. As Bryant Wood states:

Albright's theory, however, does not stand in the face of the evidence which he himself uncovered. First of all, the site was heavily fortified, which would not have been necessary had the area been used merely for an annual pilgrimage. Secondly, the numerous artifacts found lying about indicated long-term occupation — household utensils, loom-weights and spindle-whorls for spinning, and millstones for grinding grain into flour. This, plus other evidence, indicates that Bab edh-Dhra was more than a place of pilgrimage. It was a settled community, and what is more, appears to have been one of the Cities of the Plain.

Excavations At Bab edh-Dhra

Bab edh-Dhra was excavated between 1965 and 1967 by the American Schools of Oriental Research, directed by the late Paul Lapp, Bryant Wood comments further:

The total size of the cemetery at Bab edh-Dhra is mind-boggling, archaeologically speaking. In overall extent, it is more than five-eighths of a mile in length and at least half that wide. Lapp believed that the cemetery extended even farther, but he was limited in the area he could investigate because of military restrictions. More incredible than its size is the intensity of its use. The archaeologist estimated that if the rest of the cemetery is like the area investigated, it contains a minimum of 20,000 shaft tombs. Conservative estimates place the number of dead in these tombs at over half a million and the number of pottery vessels at two million.

Bryant Wood then puts the story in focus as he tells us:

"Following the untimely death of Paul Lapp in 1970, the job of publishing the Bab edh-Dhra materials fell to R. Thomas Schaub, religion professor and archaeologist from Pennsylvania State University at Middletown, Pennsylvania, and Walter E. Rast, of Valparaiso University, Valparaiso, Indiana.

As they worked on the material it became apparent that there were some basic questions about the site that remained unanswered. How is this great town site and its accompanying massive cemetery to be explained? Did people come from faraway places to utilize the area at certain times of the year as suggested by Albright? Did they bring their dead for burial at this place out of some special considerations, such as for rituals? Or was Bab edh-Dhra part of a greater system of Early Bronze sites in the area; the others, perhaps, having been inundated by the encroaching waters of the Dead Sea, as Albright and others have conjectured?

In order to find the answers to these questions, Schaub and Rast undertook a survey of the plain south of Bab Edh-Dhra (the "Ghor," or "valley"). They had some clues there might be Early Bronze Age settlements in this region. A German scholar who explored this area, Fritz Frank, published photos of tombs at Safi and Feifa which looked very much like those at Bab edh-Dhra. In addition, while visiting a small museum in Kerak in 1972, Schaub and Rast examined some pottery from Feifa which had a striking resemblance to the pottery from Bab edh-Dhra. With these hints, the two archaeologists set out on their survey in late May, 1973, unaware of the sensational discovery they were about to make.

The two archaeologists found a number of sites with tombs, underground chambers from the Early Bronze Period, and defense walls, all located near springs which could have given a sufficient water supply to the inhabitants of the particular sites.

At Feifa, Numeira, Safi, and Khanazir, they found similar patterns. It was clear that these sites, together with Bab edh-Dhra, comprised a series of five cities that had been occupied up to about the time of Abraham. At all sites early bronze pottery was found — this being the period immediately before Abraham's time. There is of course a degree of overlap between Middle and Early Bronze, as with other succeeding cultures, and this is especially so in areas that are somewhat away from the usual trade routes, as would have been the case with these particular sites, situated as they were to the east of the Dead Sea.

Evidences Of Large Population

The two archaeologists found no other Early Bronze civilizations in the area, despite their intensive search. They examined every wadi (stream) and hillock that had any possible sign of occupation.

Clearly this southern Ghor region supported an enormous population — the size of the three cemeteries established that. Albright's conclusion about a pilgrimage center must be discarded. These cities alongside the Dead Sea "were evidently joined together in an integrated system to supervise the main work supporting the economy of the area, agriculture."

An examination of the Biblical, archaeological, geographical, and geological evidence indicates that the five sites identified by Schaub and Rast are probably the five Cities of the Plain mentioned in Genesis 14.

Lot Chooses Sodom

The Bible tells of Lot choosing the Sodom area when he and Abraham separated, and Genesis 13:10-13 describes the area as being "well-watered" and "like the Garden of the Lord." Bryant Wood states:

> The Hebrew words translated "well-watered" are *kullahh*, an intensive form of the verb meaning "to be complete", and *mashqeh*, from the verb meaning "to give to drink" or "irrigate."The meaning of *kullahh mashqeh*, then is to be completely and totally irrigated.
>
> The irrigation of the southern Ghor, combined with the warm climate, resulted in a lush, tropical region that was comparable to the Garden of Eden and the fertile Nile valley in Egypt. It took a strong and efficient organization, however, to establish and maintain this irrigation system. This was the function of the five Cities of the Plain. They are referred to as a group in the Bible and were, in fact, a unified confederation, a pentapolis.

Protecting the Life-Line

Wood further elaborates:

> The source of water for the Early Bronze irrigation system in the plain was the freshwater streams flowing down from the eastern hills. And it was precisely at the point where these streams enter the Ghor ("Valley") that the Cities of the Plain were located. Thus each city could control and regulate the water flow into its area of responsibility, and also protect the source of the water, their precious life-line.

Wood goes on to point out that the Hebrew form used for the "Cities of the Plain" means in fact that the cities had some connection with the plain but were not actually in or on the plain (technically, it is in the "construct state"). This is an interesting point that fits the facts of discovery by the two archaeologists Schaub and Rast.

In this line of cities, each is near one of the separate series of water supplies, and all are built on spurs at the edge of the wadis, thus having natural defense that would command the total area. They were also in virtually equally spaced centers, giving a line of protection against any attack from the eastern highlands. All this could explain why there was a road, known even in Roman times, which is still visible in photographs taken from the air. It extends to the edge of the Dead Sea on the western side and then continues on the eastern side. Apparently access to these cities was much easier in the days of Abraham before the "Valley of Siddim" became "The Salt Sea."

Both the geological and the archaeological evidence would allow the identification of these five sites as the "Cities of the Plain". It is usually accepted that the destruction was caused by earthquake activity which resulted in combustible materials being erupted from the earth's surface. The five sites now identified lie at the edge of the Ghor, right along the eastern fault line, east of the southern portion of the Dead Sea.

The archaeologists Schaub and Rast found evidence that at least two of the sites (Numeira and Feifa) had been burned — "they were able to scoop up charcoal directly from the surface at both sites."

The available evidence thus points to these five Early Bronze sites being the Biblical Cities of the Plain. The Bible even gives certain clues by which the cities themselves might be identified. Wood states:

> We will start with Zoar, since this was the only one of the five cities to survive the

calamity. Because Lot wished to flee to Zoar rather than the mountains, the Lord promised, 'I will not overthrow this city' (Genesis 19:21). This is further substantiated by Deuteronomy 29:23 where Zoar is absent from the list of the Cities of the Plain that were destroyed. Of the five cities, Zoar is the only one that is later referred to in the Bible as still existing (Deuteronomy 34:3, Isaiah 15:5, and Jeremiah 48:34). Later historians occasionally spoke of Zoar, and the name has survived to this day in connection with the remains of successive towns around the mouth of the Wadi Hesa. It was near these remains that the Early Bronze site was found by Schaub and Rast. We can be fairly confident, then, that the Early Bronze site at Safi was ancient Zoar.

Another clue is the fact that the four destroyed cities are always mentioned in pairs. In Deuteronomy 29:23 the names Sodom and Gomorrah are connected by the Hebrew conjunction "waw" as are the names Admah and Zeboim. Sodom and Gomorrah appear together as a pair in many passages throughout the Bible. Admah and Zeboim appear together again in Hosea 11:8. It would seem logical, then, that Sodom was located next to Gomorrah and Admah next to Zeboim. Since Zoar conveniently falls in the centre of the five cities, one pair of names can be assigned to the two sites north of Zoar and the other pair to the south of Zoar. But which is which?

A third clue in identifying the sites is a description of the Canaanite border given in Genesis 10:19: "And the border of the Canaanites was from Sidon, as thou comest to Gerar, unto Gaza; as thou goest, unto Sodom and Gomorrah, and Admah, and Zeboim, even unto Lasha." Beginning at Sidon on the northern Mediterranean coast, the border is traced south to Gaza and then east to Sodom. If we assume that from Sodom the border is being traced in the northerly direction, and that the cities are named in south-to-north order, we have the identification of each site! The border goes from Sodom to Gomorrah to Admah to Zeboim. From Zeboim, the boundary line then goes to Lasha. The exact location of Lasha is not certain. It may be the same as Leshem in Joshua 19:47 and Laishah in Judges 18:29 and thereby may be equated to Dan in northern Israel. At any rate, in order to complete the specification of the Canaanite territory, the border must have proceeded north from Zeboim.

The placing of the cities in the south-to-north order of Sodom, Gomorrah, Admah, and Zeboim matches the Sodom-Gomorrah, Admah-Zeboim pairing noted previously. In addition, Sodom seems to be given prominence among the five cities as this is the one most often mentioned in the Bible. This fits our proposed identification, as the southernmost city would have had to be well fortified and well garrisoned in order to protect the southern boundary of the plain.

Our suggested identification with the five Early Bronze sites then is: Khanazir — Sodom, Feifa — Gomorrah, Safi — Zoar, Numeira — Admah, and Bab edh-Dhra — Zeboim.

One final check we can make on our identification is the length of time it took Lot to flee from Sodom to Zoar. At dawn, the angels hustled Lot and his family out of Sodom

(Genesis 19:15). When they arrived in Zoar, the sun had risen over the land (Genesis 19:23). So we can estimate that the journey took a matter of a few hours. The distance from Khanazir to Feifa is about 6 kilometres, or 3.7 miles, and from Feifa to Safi is about 10 kilometres, or 6.2 miles. The total journey, then, was about 10 miles. For people fleeing destruction, it would have been no difficulty to cover 10 miles in a matter of a few hours. (Except someone who was reluctant to leave, such as Lot's wife!)

We can say in summary that all of the evidence we have in hand at this time points to the identification of the Early Bronze sites discovered by Schaub and Rast as Sodom, Gomorrah, and the Cities of the Plain. Although they are cautious about identifying the ruins as the Cities of the Plain, scholars seem to feel that the conclusion is almost unavoidable. "These are the only candidates we have," said Schaub in an interview.

Professor G. Ernest Wright, of Harvard University, who is also President of the American Schools of Oriental Research, agreed: "As you go around the Dead Sea and look for an historical setting for Genesis 14 and 19, this is the only area it could be," he said.

Bryant Wood goes on to discuss life in the Cities of the Plain. The evidence suggests that the communities were highly organized, with complex irrigation systems maintained. Possibly there was no family life as we know it, a communal life being practiced, and the people were very prosperous. In the main they followed agricultural pursuits, but there were subsidiary occupations, even including tomb-cutting, and high-class pottery making. There were also religious cultic personnel, and their religious practices bore similarities to what is known of the practices of other peoples of this time.

Conclusion

It seems that the five "Cities of the Plain" have been found. In his *Bible and Spade* article, Bryant Wood even shows a photograph of a heap of stones which might prove to be the gate at Sodom where Lot sat.

It is interesting to realize that the acceptance of this point of view means that even this author (Clifford Wilson) has necessarily discarded a previous viewpoint. In the earlier editions of *Crash Go The Chariots*, the theory was accepted that the cities of Sodom and Gomorrah were buried beneath the southern part of the Dead Sea; but this is now unlikely. The new identification means that an earlier theory must be discarded. This is of real significance as far as Biblical accuracy and background are concerned. As Bryant Wood so capably demonstrates, the Bible record gives certain clues to the location of these cities, and some of those clues were hidden within the grammatical constructions of the text.

It is relevant to point out that the discarding of old theories does take place from time to time, and they are not "cemented down" as von Daniken suggests in regard to archaeological theories. Archaeologists have been prepared to think again on such matters as Solomon's stables at Megiddo (they should be dated later), and the situation of Jerusalem's walls in the days of David. The fact is, archaeologists are prepared to modify their conclusions and even to put them aside if factual evidence demonstrates that earlier theories can no longer be supported.

Interestingly enough, it is also relevant to state that the Bible did not say that the cities of Sodom and Gomorrah were beneath the waters of the southern part of the Dead Sea. The theory was interesting, but it was merely an interpretation. The Bible record itself continues to stand as such theories come and go. For this reason, the historical validity of the Bible must not be allowed to stand simply on the evidence of archaeology. Archaeologists can be wrong, and at times they are. The amazing thing is that, despite the changes in theories, the Bible is proved to be right all the time.

No Atomic Blast After All!

Much of what we have said is in direct opposition to the theory of Erich von Daniken that the Cities of the Plain were destroyed by atomic blast. He suggested that a group of divers should investigate the Dead Sea "for radioactive traces of an atomic explosion over Sodom and Gomorrah" (p. 45).

This implies his acceptance of the theory that the cities of Sodom and Gomorrah are buried beneath the southern part of the Dead Sea. Actually, divers have already looked for evidences of the cities under the water, and they were not successful. This is to be expected if the new knowledge referred to earlier in this chapter is factual — as it seems to be.

Von Daniken develops his hypothesis at some length, with the angelic messengers having to hurry Lot and his family out of the doomed city because the countdown had already begun (p. 53), with Lot's wife soon destroyed because of the effects of radiation when she looked back. According to von Daniken, "Lot's wife turned round and looked straight at the atomic sun. Nowadays no one is surprised that she fell dead on the spot" (p. 54).

Various points can be made against von Daniken's hypothesis. The very fact that this series of cemeteries has been found, associated with five cities, indicates that people buried their dead. If the cities were destroyed by an atomic explosion, who was there to do the burying of the last generation of citizens? The burials point to settled civilization over a long period of time.

Contrary to von Daniken's argument that the countdown had already begun (p. 53), and that the angels were hurrying them out, the Bible record actually states that the destruction would not come until Lot had escaped. Lot and his family were being given a final opportunity to remove themselves from a situation in which it seems that spiritually they should not have been involved. Lot had selfishly chosen the "best" at a time when his men fell out with the employees of Abraham, and he had "set his tent toward Sodom." Eventually he was actually sitting in the gate, a highly respected member of the Sodom community, a city that was clearly identified with depravity (so much so that the very name "Sodom" has become a byword through the centuries).

As for von Daniken's theory about Lot's wife turning around and looking straight at the atomic sun (p. 54), the Hebrew term indicates that this was no casual glance, but a fixed staring. Her heart was still in Sodom even in this twelfth-hour deliverance.

Von Daniken suggests that we are less credulous than our fathers and so "we cannot imagine an omnipotent, ubiquitous, infinitely good God who is above all concepts of time and yet does not know what is going to happen." (p. 54). There is nothing in the Bible text relating to the destruction of the cities of Sodom and Gomorrah indicating that God did not know what was going to happen. God has not created man to be a robot, for man is a creature with free will. Lot was free to escape or not to escape, and this was true of his wife also. Lot's wife took the first reluctant steps, but did not carry through. She paid the price of her own folly.

The Geologist Speaks

It is probable that there is a natural explanation, in the overruling of God, for the great destruction that took place at this time. Geologists tell us that there are still great deposits of salt, sulphur, and bitumen in this area of the Dead Sea, and also that the bubbles of natural gas, which keep on escaping, point to oil deposits.

The entire area is in the Great Rift Valley which extends from Mt. Hermon in the north through to the Lakes system in Africa. In the southern Dead Sea area, this rift is about 1,300 feet below the level of the Mediterranean Sea; the northern part of the Dead Sea is yet another 1,300 feet deeper. Little wonder this rift is called "The Great Rift Valley."

Alongside the Dead Sea area there are great cracks, or "faults," as they are called by geologists; consequently, earth tremors occur there frequently.

Alongside the southern part of the Dead Sea is a mountain called Jebel Usdum, which is Arabic for Mt. Sodom. The salt at its base is 150 feet deep over a distance of several miles. High up on this mountain there are clear evidences of a violent eruption, for the various strata of the earth's surface are found welded together as though by intense heat. It seems that the salt, the sulphur, and the bitumen were hurled into the air when the great oil basin beneath the southern part of the Dead Sea was disturbed, probably by an earthquake, and natural gases were ignited after they escaped into the atmosphere. The marl, as it is called, high up on Mt. Sodom, is clear evidence of a violent eruption as great quantities of the earth's surface were hurled up the mountainside.

Another point is that the word translated "brimstone" actually means "bituminous material," and highly inflammable bitumen is very plentiful in the area. This is also referred to in the Bible, in Genesis 14, verse 10.

A reconstruction could involve an extensive area, and we have seen that at least one of the sites identified as the "Cities of the Plain" gives evidence of intense burning. Earlier evidence came from the surface surveys by Professor Nelson Glueck of the sites alongside the Dead Sea. He pointed out that the general area had been inhabited spasmodically up to about the 19th century B.C., but was then not extensively settled again for several centuries.

What About Lot's Wife?

The question might be asked, "What about Lot's wife? Do you really believe the story about the pillar of salt?" The answer, of course, is yes. If people in Pompeii could be overcome by volcanic lava, why could not a woman fleeing from Sodom be overcome by rock salt? Pillars of salt are plentiful in the area, and one 40-foot pillar is known as "Lot's Wife." We do not suggest that this really does enclose Lot's wife, but it is evidence of a tradition that a woman was so enclosed. She certainly could have been, for the salt was 150 feet deep in this area — and this great layer of salt was fractured with the other strata of the earth's surface and hurled into the air.

The Smoke, Not the Fire

An interesting and relevant point is found in Genesis 19:28, which tells us that Abraham looked and saw the smoke ascending as the smoke of a furnace. Abraham was at Hebron, and there were mountain ridges between Hebron and Sodom. He could not have seen the fire itself, but he saw the smoke high in the sky. Abraham saw the smoke, we are told, and there is no mention of his seeing the fire. This seemingly casual statement implies there was an eye-witness account of this record.

A Brief Scientific Reconstruction

Briefly then, it seems likely that at the time of this divine judgment an earthquake ground up rocks at the edge of the geological fault and natural gases from the underlying oil field carried many of these rocks, together with salt, sulphur, and bitumen, high into the air. The natural gases ignited, and fire and bitumen literally rained from the sky.

The archaeological evidence, geological evidence, and other pointers come together to show clearly that the Biblical description of the destruction of the cities of Sodom and Gomorrah can be substantiated by an acceptable reconstruction. This is not to say that there is no possibility that symbolic language is not included in the text. The popular idea of fire and brimstone simply raining from heaven is not endorsed by the reconstruction in this book. God, Who controls the universe, also controls the timing of natural events; it is possible that the miraculous events on this occasion included a simultaneous ignition of an oil well. The fact is, the Bible does not speak of an atomic explosion, even though Erich von Daniken has enough imagination to find one at Sodom. The reconstruction that we have presented is perfectly acceptable "scientifically," and is compatible with the Bible record. Talk of an atomic explosion is pure fantasy.

Yet another "Chariot" has crashed, plunging into those Moabite foothills alongside the Dead Sea.

6

Here, There, and Everywhere
An Ancient Map . . .
Venus . . . Carbon Dating

Anyone reading *Chariots of the Gods?* soon finds that the author jumps from subject to subject, culture to culture, extravagant claim to unsupported conclusions. His writing is something of a literary maze. Thus, a systematic analysis of his work is difficult to confine to a few chapters. In this chapter, therefore, we consider a number of subjects as we briefly explain why we reject his hypothesis at particular points.

Piri Reis and That Ancient Map of the World

The author of *Chariots* uses some ancient maps to bolster his hypothesis of visits of gods from space. These maps had belonged to a Turkish Naval Officer who was known as Piri Re'is (Re'is means Admiral).

One map especially has been singled out, for it was supposed to be part of a map of the world taken from a very great height (p. 30). According to von

Daniken, this 16th century map was virtually identical with one taken from a space-ship hovering over Cairo. To prove his point the map is included in *Chariots*, together with other pictures in the central part of the book. It takes some effort to be able to fit the Piri Re'is map onto the one taken over Cairo, and as von Daniken himself states, the various countries must be re-shuffled to make them fit (p. 29). However, having done this preliminary juggling, he claims they are "fantastically accurate" (p. 30). The hypothesis is then put forward by the author of *Chariots* that they must have been taken from a high-flying aircraft or from a spaceship (p. 31).

Piri Re'is himself stated on the map in question that he had consulted 20 different earlier charts in the preparation of his own work. These were maps that ranged over approximately two thousand years. One interesting sidelight is that the River Amazon is shown twice on the Admiral's map, which can probably be explained by the fact that it WAS a piecing together of a number of charts, meticulously drawn, but still coming from widely different sources.

Though the map is indeed a remarkable achievement of the Renaissance period, it is not as accurate as is claimed by von Daniken. Nearly a thousand miles of coast is missing from east South America, and what he claims is Antarctica is a land mass joined directly to South America — the ocean between is ignored. A space photograph certainly would not produce such a result.

It is at least debatable to suggest that an aerial photograph over Cairo could ever include the Antarctic Continent. Nor would an actual photograph make a total error of about five per cent in the size of the land masses.

The Piri Re'is work is highly creditable, being a

painstaking attempt to correct the known efforts of the cartographers before him. We do well to accept his own statement that he consulted 20 other charts in the preparation of this new map — but he did NOT take a journey in a spaceship!

Were "Animal Gods" Worshipped and Eaten?

Whether it is absurd or not, it is fact. Ancient Egyptians worshipped bulls and other animals, as well as edible birds and fish which were the symbols of various gods. The Canaanites, the Babylonians, the Assyrians all revered the bull, but this did not prevent their feasting on it.

All the gods who are depicted in cave drawings in Sweden and Norway have uniform undefinable heads. The archaeologists say that they are animal heads. Yet isn't there something rather absurd about worshipping a "god" whom one also slaughters and eats? (p. 49).

Furnaces With Air Channels At Ezion-Geber

Erich von Daniken refers to the earlier held view that at Ezion-Geber some of the buildings were smelting installations "consisting of a regular ultra-modern furnace with a system of air channels, chimney flues, and openings for specific purposes" (p. 62).

The archaeologists whom he brands as inflexible have long ago recognized that these "smelting installations" were in fact storerooms. Smelting did take place in the area, but the interpretation as to the controlled air channels, put out by Professor Nelson Glueck, has been withdrawn. The author of *Chariots* is not up to date at this point; nor is he accurate when he says that, "All these finds are estimated to be at least 5,000 years old!"(p. 62). Some were dated to about 1,000 B.C. — approximately 3,000 years ago. Nor is copper sulphate that from which copper is obtained — it comes from sulphide minerals. Perhaps these space charioteers, with their advanced techniques, had missed out on learning this particular one!

This is another clear example of archaeologists who are prepared to meet the facts and to change strongly-held viewpoints, as was the case with this widely-publicized theory. The consistent adaptation displayed as new discoveries are made hardly fits the cynical approach of von Daniken toward archaeologists.

A Fireball In 1500 B.C.

Sometimes the points that von Daniken raises are so weak as supports to his argument that a discerning reader almost feels like saying, "So what?" One such case is that of a text from the time of the Egyptian Pharaoh Tuthmosis III, telling of a ball of fire with an evil smell — the Pharaoh and his men watched it until it rose in a southerly direction and disappeared from view (p. 80).

A fireball was witnessed by several members of the Church of which I was a member in Malvern, Victoria, Australia. It came through the ceiling, roared through the church, then disappeared out the window. Was it the exhaust of a space chariot? Of course not! But if imagination is allowed to run riot there could be a wonderful story to tell. The point is, a report from an Egyptian about a fireball in ancient times is hardly sufficient evidence to substantiate a visit from a space craft.

It is relevant to point out that we are not debating the possibilities of UFOs. In fact, in a further book written since *Crash Go The Chariots* was first published, *UFOs And Their Mission Impossible*, we make it very clear that such phenomena must be taken seriously. We analyze the various possible explanations, and finally come to the two basic alternatives — "invasion" by beings from another planet, utilizing anti-gravitational beams and electromagnetic force; or the paraphysical explanation, which at first sight might seem "way-out" but is basically endorsed by the official United States investigation headed by the late Dr. E.U. Condon (the Condon Report was issued in 1969). Many reputable scientists read it, eventually accepted it, but then backed off from the subject because they did not want to be involved with an explanation that put UFOs in a somewhat similar category as seances and beings from the spirit world. Nevertheless, the evidence is of such a nature that it must be taken seriously — hence the book, *UFOs And Their Mission Impossible.*

Those Ancient Water Tunnels

On page 36 in *Chariots of the Gods?* von Daniken tells us about water tunnels at Tiahuanaco, constructed with "such precision that our modern concrete conduits seem the work of mere bunglers in comparison." This sort of statement is supposed to impress on us that only technicians with the sort of know-how associated with visitors from space could have made them.

The argument is again quite unconvincing. Anybody who has waded through that amazing conduit of Hezekiah underneath the walls of ancient Jerusalem (as I have done) must acknowledge that some of these men of old had the great technical know-how to construct their extensive conduits. The ruins of the one built by Herod the Great from Mount Carmel to the sea are still amazing. This conduit was a "double-header" — two tunnels, one on top of the other. The ruins can be seen at Caesarea. However, Herod and Hezekiah certainly did not claim the help of astronauts for the building of these ancient marvels.

Did the World Float on an Elephant?

One of the drawings opposite page 97 of *Chariots*

shows a man in some sort of a vessel, with others outside, possibly in an attitude of worship. The structure is borne up by two men who are in turn on the back of an animal that looks like an elongated cat. We are not told the significance, as it is simply included with "More ancient drawings — from *Navoy.*" Possibly it is meant to convey the idea that a visitor from outer space came in such a vessel, for what looks like the rays of the sun surround it, and two of the other pictures on the page speak about men in space suits.

One Hindu story tells of the world's being held in place on the back of a huge elephant (plus a tortoise, etc.). If such drawings as this opposite page 97 are to be used as serious argument, it is reasonable to assume that the elephant story must also be taken seriously.

The Teaching of a Simple Language

At page 26 we learn of people using their "simple language" to put in sage form the visit of the gods.

There is no such thing as a simple language. Linguists of this generation have established that all known languages are very complex. Earlier generations had thought that primitive peoples would have simple languages, but this has not proved to be the case. The complexities of human language are great whether one is dealing with "educated" people or those who know little of modern civilization.

Written communications have developed from simple to more complex forms, but this is not so with speech. However, according to von Daniken, those "primitive" people were able to pass on the details of the visit from space (p. 82). They understood the language of the gods, and believed their promise of a return (p. 103). They are supposed to have known that "the body cells (can) continue to live, slowed down a billionfold after special treatment" (p. 105).

This certainly does not suggest that such people had only a simple language, but rather that it was complex, and that they had knowledge which only now are we beginning to re-discover. Clearly, these were not the simple people von Daniken hypothesizes! They appear rather to have been transported by some time machine into the 21st century A.D.

Venus and von Daniken

It is commonplace that many enthusiasts thought that life might exist on the planet Venus, but as von Daniken himself acknowledges (p. 151), that theory is no longer held because of the very high temperatures on its surface.

However, our special interest in von Daniken's theory is that he discusses the viewpoint of Dr. Emanuel Velikovsky in *Worlds in Collision* — on which I am touching only insofar as it is relevant to this analysis. Von Daniken states that Velikovsky's theory regarding the formation of Venus is confirmed by the results from the spacecraft Mariner II. As Velikovsky associates this with the action that caused the Red Sea to open when the Israelites crossed it in the days of Moses, it follows that Venus could not have been in existence until less than three and a half thousand years ago.

The relevance to von Daniken is that elsewhere he makes the following statement:

In the mountainous Asian region of Kohistan a cave drawing reproduces the exact position of the constellations as they actually were 10,000 years ago, Venus and the earth are joined by lines (p. 43).

So which IS true? If Venus was formed 3 to 4 thousand years ago it certainly was not there 10,000 years ago. This seems to be yet another contradic-

"They Will Never Be On Show In a Museum"

Referring to the huge colossi of the Olmecs of Mexico, von Daniken states that "they will never be on show in a museum" (p. 117). He goes on to state, "No bridge in the country could stand the weight."

Gordon Whittaker (in *Some Trust in Chariots*, p. 51) points out that some of these giant heads ARE found in museums, and that "one was recently transported thousands of miles to the Metropolitan Museum of Art in New York for a special exhibition."

Whittaker is an authority on Aztec culture. He goes on to "punch holes" in a whole series of *Chariot* myths, one other interesting example being that of von Daniken's helmeted spacemen at the Toltec capital. These actually are Toltec soldiers wearing headdresses and protective breastplates. Their pieces of "communications equipment" are nothing more than spear throwers.

That Cloth From Helwan

Another von Daniken "evidence" of visitors from outer space is that at Helwan there is a piece of cloth with fabric so fine that today it could only be woven "in a special factory with great technical knowhow and experience" (p. 43).

Equally impressive woven fabrics are known much earlier, as textbooks and museums make clear. Not only have beautifully woven fabrics many centuries older than this particular cloth come down to us, but also ancient looms themselves have been preserved for posterity. Von Daniken's sensationalism is again unjustified.

The So-Called "Elephant Island" In the River Nile

A lady who read the first edition of *Crash Go The Chariots* commented, "It's convincing — but I'd still like to know about the 'elephant shaped island.'" I had not thought it specially significant, but others also might ask questions, so here is a comment.

Von Daniken states that even in the older texts this island in the middle of the Nile was called "Elephantine" because it always resembled an elephant, and he asks, "But how did the ancient Egyptians know that, because this shape can only be recognized from a plane at a great height?" (p. 85).

The Greek word "elephantinos" does not mean "elephant," but "ivory." It is itself a translation of the Egyptian word "Yeb," and the island of Yeb is known before the times of the Greeks, who called it "Elephantine."

Secondly, the island does not resemble the shape of an elephant today, as is implied in *Chariots*. Even if it did (which the maps negate), this would argue more against von Daniken's claim than for it, for relatively small river islands may change their shape over long periods.

David's Fight With a Six-Fingered Giant

Von Daniken suggests the need to "query our Old Testament dating" (p. 59) because of the incident recorded at II Sameul, chapter 21, where David fights with a giant who had six fingers and six toes.

There is no need to query our dating because of this incident, for it is not merely associated with giants of ancient times. Giantism has been known in both ancient and modern times. Nor should there be any real problem about believing that the giant had six fingers and six toes. We quote from *The Wycliffe Bible Commentary*, at p. 304:

"Six fingers. . .six toes" — This was not an unusual deformity in ancient times, nor is it in modern times. Pliny mentioned such a peculiarity in his *Natural History*. According to Leviticus 21:18 one with such a deformity was excluded from the temple service.

Years ago I was lecturing on this part of the Old Testament at the Melbourne Bible Institute in Australia. I carefully researched this incident and discovered the interesting fact that one of the kings of England had the same deformity. I must have seemed a little defensive to some members of the class, for suddenly I noticed a hand go up — of a very courteous young lady! She was a qualified nursing sister. I stopped, and asked what she wanted.

"My sister was born with six toes on both feet," she said. It turned out that others were able to make a contribution which made it clear that the condition exists today. There should be no problem accepting this fact of Bible history, despite von Daniken's suggestion of the need to "query our Old Testament dating."

"What Titanic Force Turned It Upside Down"

Von Daniken refers to a huge block at Sacsayhuaman in Peru, and asks, "What titanic force turned it upside down?"

One possible answer is that an earthquake turned it upside down, for the area is in a great earthquake chain of South America. We do not need "titanic forces" to explain earthquake damage today, and we certainly do not need to look to von Daniken's "titanic forces" to explain such happenings in the past.

Even if this were not in an earthquake region (as it is), von Daniken's space-gods would not be needed to turn a huge block over. J. Eric S. Thompson in *The Rise and Fall of Maya Civilization* has an interesting comment, indirectly relevant. It seems that after the overthrow of the rulers at Tikal in Guatemala, the masons were won over to the rebels and they attempted a measure of restoration, and:

At Tikal broken stelae were reset, even upside down (p. 106).

This was not in Peru, but away to the north in Central America. It demonstrates that sometimes monuments were reset upside down by human, not astronaut force.

Incidentally, the heaviest stone at Sacsayhuaman is calculated to be about 200 tons, and this stone is pointed out as being the heaviest of all those used by the Incas. It is common for people to have their photographs taken standing alongside it, and the stone is about 12 feet in height. Von Daniken speaks of the stone at Sacsayhuaman as being 20,000 tons but suggests that it is in a secret place, half a mile away from the well-known Inca fortress. When I interviewed Reverend Donald Bond, who has been a Missionary in Peru for over 15 years, he stated that he had personally stood a man alongside this famous stone at Sacsayhuaman; but in his 15 years as a Missionary in Peru he has never heard of this secret Sacsayhuaman to which Erich von Daniken refers. He went on to state that there was no mystery about the stone that weighed 200 tons, as the Incas had vast manpower resources, and that certainly space machines had not been needed in ancient times to move the stones that were quarried about three miles from the fort at Sacsayhuaman. They were simply rolled along on huge wooden rollers, a relatively easy process.

Perhaps it should be also stated that there are huge stones incorporated in various ancient constructions, such as the Mortuary Temple of Mycerinus and the Temple of Solomon. These occasional megaliths have made it clear that not only were huge slabs lifted and transported, but also they were placed in their appointed positions . . . without astronauts!

Additionally, von Daniken stated that the Incas had no weaving; his implication is that they were taught by astronauts. However, the fact is that the

Incas were famous for their weaving. They utilized fine cotton cloths that were beautifully colored with inks and dyes. In fact, the different cultures in the various areas became distinguished by their particular cloths with their distinctive weaving patterns. One of the ways in which it was possible to tell one age from another was by the type of weaving and the figures used in the weaving. Experts say that some of the early weaving of the Inca people was exceptionally good, some of the best ever found in the world.

The Indian Pillar That Does Not Rust

Von Daniken's book shows a picture of an old Indian pillar in the center section. The caption tells us that the iron in this pillar does not rust, and that the pillar is hundreds of years old.

This pillar is situated at Delhi and the story of its "special" qualities is well known. It is regarded by many people as a lucky charm, and some scholars suggest that the constant placing of sweaty hands on its sides helps to prevent rust. However (despite von Daniken's claim to the contrary on page 44), it is NOT rust-proof, for it does contain phosphorus and does show signs of some rust, though it is true that it is remarkably well preserved. Such a phenomenon does not, however, point to some special technique introduced by astronaut gods, any more than the fact that some other techniques known to ancient people have surprised modern scholars.

Since the publication of the original edition of *Crash Go The Chariots* I have had evidence sent to me that "bob iron" mined in New Jersey is of similar quality to that in the Indian pillar at Delhi. The people in that area, however, have no knowledge of astronauts ever conducting mining operations there!

It is relevant at this point to say that there are

many techniques that we still do not fully understand. When I was associated with the Austrialian Institute of Archaeology, we received into our collection an original bronze figure of the god Baal. It had a leg missing, and we had a modern one added. The metallurgists told us the original was harder than they could make — to their surprise.

Since writing the original edition of *Crash Go The Chariots* there has been yet another note to this story. I again met one of those metallurgists and he told me he had a solution to this particular problem. It has been found that Japanese Samurrai swords have the same strange hardening. This is done by hammering the blade to paper thickness, and then hammering it back again. As this process is repeated changes take place in the molecular structure of the steel and unusual hardening results. He assured me that this would answer the problem of the strange hardness of the Baal figure.

Many other examples can be cited of advanced techniques being known to people of long ago — witness the magnificent gold vessels from Ur, dating to about 2,500 B.C. Their two-storied houses also surprised the excavators. This in no way suggests a visit from space, but simply indicates that technical knowledge was more advanced than we of the 20th century would have expected.

The famous iron pillar to which von Daniken refers is in the same category.

The Mayas Of Central America

Another group to whom von Daniken refers is that people known as the Mayas of Central America. He hypothesizes that they made calculations by means of an electronic brain (p. 76). This view is not that generally held by archaeologists, but we have already pointed out that this does not especially concern von Daniken, who sets himself up as an authority beyond accepted scholarship.

Nevertheless, it should be stated that archaeologists do not credit these early Central Americans with established writing until about the 5th century A.D. Even if writing were known when their civilization is believed to have commenced, about a thousand years earlier, it does not seem plausible that this group would have had knowledge of astronomical details that could be accurately dated back 27,000 years.

That "Miracle" Jade From China

One continues to read on about these fantastic Latin American sites, all the more amazing because of the seeming new knowledge available to von Daniken. Thus at pages 116-117 we learn another fact about this Mayan civilization:

The fantastic five-strand necklace of green jade in the burial pyramid of Tikal in Guatemala is a miracle. A miracle because the jade comes from China.

Actually it should not be a miracle even by von Daniken's own arguments, for if the Babylonian "Epic of Gilgamesh" could originate from South America as he hypothesizes (p. 69), why could not jade have been imported from China? So where is the miracle?

The fact is, jade is readily plentiful in the river beds and mountains of Latin America. Here are two brief selections from Thomas Gann's *Maya Cities*.

Around this skeleton (of a young child — Ed.) were scattered broadcast a large handful of pieces of jade, some crude and unpolished, others partly worked, and others apparently fragments of broken ornaments (p. 89 and 195).

With the skull (of a young adult — Ed.) in the northernmost temple was found a small necklace of very fine jade beads (p. 198).

We read of jade used as ear plugs (p. 242) and to plug holes in teeth! (p. 243).

One need only consult the references to "jade" in J. Eric S. Thompson's *Rise and Fall of Maya Civilization* to realize that it was relatively plentiful. This quotation is from that source:

> Equally valuable was jade. One ancient work site of the mineral has been found in the Sierra de Las Minas in the north-eastern highlands, and no doubt others will be located. Jade was a symbol of wealth but also had religious associations. For instance, a jade bead was frequently placed in the mouth of a dead person of rank. Jades were offered in sacrifice and used in divination (pp. 20-21).

One chief was found with a magnificent mask consisting of two hundred pieces of jade arranged over his face and a jade ring on each finger. There were also necklaces and wrist pieces, the total count of jade pieces in that one tomb being 978! (p. 79).

Of course, J. Eric S. Thompson writes as an archaeologist, and we have already seen von Daniken's opinion of archaeologists. How many "Chinese miracles" must there have been amongst those ancient Mayas? Or is it that another chariot has crashed into the mountains and rivers of Latin America?

Radio Carbon Dating

A subject touched on briefly by Erich von Daniken is radio carbon dating. This theory is not now as "popular" as it was, and dating by this and similar methods has become suspect. When carbon dating was first announced by Dr. Libby in 1949, it was thought to be the last word; but that early confidence has been replaced by a sense of caution.

Carbon dating can be shown to be relatively accurate for one half-life, that is, approximately five and a half thousand years, for there are written records that can be put alongside dates for that time. Beyond that period dating is an open question, for there simply are not absolutes against which specific dates can be fixed with accuracy.

There are great problems even with dates within one half-life, not only with carbon dating, but also with other systems involving radiometric processes as well. One example is a date of thousands of years given to lava rocks in Hawaii; they are known to be less than 200 years old.

However, some of these dates have also opened up new areas of challenging investigation. Why are Carbon-14 dates possible for oil deposits and even for coal formations? By usual explanations both of these should be so old that a Carbon-14 date (that, according to the experts, can be taken for only about 60,000 with any acceptance) is out of the question. However, there are now so many dates of this nature that some of those traditional long dates are beginning to be challenged. It is now being seriously argued that the earth is not as old as "traditional" geologists have believed.

In a way, this material is an aside. One point we are making is that von Daniken accepts the system when it suits him, but not otherwise. On page 110 he refers to "the omnipotent carbon isotope C-14," and is content to accept carbon dating as accurate, for he uses it to give a comparison with a date relating to Egypt. Actually, his comparison can easily be shown not to be valid, for the figures he quotes as agreeing "pretty well" with those given by ancient Egyptian priests work out to be over 3,000 years more than the 10,400 he quotes. His own mathematics can be challenged, but the point we are making is that he accepts Carbon-14 as a dating method when he wants to "establish" his case.

Yet we go over to page 112 and become further confused by his contradictory statements. We quote:

Our hitherto existing methods of dating, including the famous carbon isotope C-14, which makes everyone so happy, leave great gaps as soon as we come to an age of more than 45,600 years.

"Everyone Happy" or "Unreliable"

We have already commented that there are no "absolutes" for comparison beyond one half-life, approximately five and a half thousand years. However, we read that von Daniken says that this dating method "makes everyone so happy." What ARE we to believe? On the same page he says, "Even recognized scholars have told me that they considered the C-14 method rather unreliable . . . ." and "These critical voices should only be accepted with limitations . . . ."

We have stated that we, too, have reservations about carbon dating — as do many scholars — and to that extent we agree with von Daniken. However, is it a satisfactory method of research to accept its evidence when the figures agree with a theory, but to accept it at other points only with limitations? Is it logical to say, it "makes everyone happy" and then immediately in the same paragraph to state that "recognized scholars" have told him that they consider the method unreliable?

This is but one piece of evidence of a number which von Daniken selects to further his arguments; and, a method is acceptable or unacceptable according to whether it fits the preconceived theory. Scientific investigation and the research methods of modern academic inquiry demand that ALL evidence be examined impartially. A method cannot be recommended or utilized at one point and then rejected if it happens not to fit a preconceived hypothesis.

Ezekiel's Space Vehicle

According to von Daniken, the "vehicle" that

Ezekiel saw was a space chariot, and the gods "took him with them in their vehicle" (p. 57). Ezekiel could not have been in touch with an almighty God, according to von Daniken, for "this kind of locomotion seems to me to be quite incompatible with the idea of an almighty God" (p. 57).

If we take the Bible record at face value, we do not find the problem insuperable after all. In the very first verse of his prophecy, Ezekiel says that he saw "visions from God." "Visions" are not necessarily literal phenomena, and in fact the descriptions that follow cannot all be taken literally in our physical sense. Ezekiel shows that the "vehicle" moves in all directions at once (chapter 1, verse 17), and instead of this being one of von Daniken's "space chariots" it is in fact a symbolic presentation, telling us that he is in touch with that Transcendent One Who is not limited by space or gravity. He was not confined to a "space chariot," but was above it (e.g., chapter 1, verse 25).

Ezekiel's prophecy includes much symbolic teaching; e.g., the Valley of Dry Bones in chapter 37. Even Ezekiel himself is told that he personally is a living symbol (Ezekiel 12:11) — he is a living symbol of the fact that the people are to go into exile, a prophecy which was literally fulfilled.

In view of the clear statements as to the symbolic elements and the visionary presentation of this prophecy, there is little point in further following the outlandish interpretations given in *Chariots* as to the experiences of Ezekiel. Von Daniken's Ezekiel chariot crashes in the mists of a visionary hypothesis.

About the Dead Sea Scrolls

Another von Daniken inaccuracy is seen in his reference to *The Apocalypse of Moses* on p. 60. He refers to this among "hitherto unknown texts" before the finding of the Dead Sea Scrolls.

However, this particular text has been widely known for several centuries. It is typical of the documents put out by Jewish writers about the time of the New Testament. Such "pseudepigraphic" writings took the name of a recognized authority in order to gain greater acceptance. Scholars do NOT regard *The Apocalypse of Moses* as serious history, nor do they regard it as genuinely coming from the hand of Moses.

In the same context, von Daniken brings two scrolls together, though he uses the name of only one, the so-called *Lamech Scroll*, an erroneous title which scholars have long since discarded in favor of *The Genesis Apocryphon*. Von Daniken brings together part of this writing, and the pseudepigraphic *Book of Enoch*, and speaks of "the astonishing . . . information" (p. 61) told to Noah's parents about the coming flood. However, both these writings are known to date to approximately New Testament times. We note again that many such writings are claimed to come from great men of the past in an attempt to gain greater favor for them. We certainly do not have here new "information" given to Noah.

From none of the Dead Sea Scrolls does von Daniken produce genuinely new evidence. He continues to confuse issues by combining fact with distortion as he attempts to bolster his own predetermined hypotheses. Much of the material to which von Daniken refers at this point is in the same category and thus does not in any way compare to the Biblical book of Genesis for being accepted as fact.

Enoch In a Fiery Chariot

We have just referred to the Book of Genesis, with which the Bible commences. Von Daniken refers to another incident recorded in that book — the transporting of Enoch to heaven. Von Daniken's wording is that Enoch "according to tradition, disappeared forever in a fiery heavenly chariot" (p. 61). This adds considerably to the Bible account, which simply says,

And Enoch walked with God: and he was not; for God took him (Genesis 5:24).

Where is the "fiery heavenly chariot?" There is an apocryphal non-Biblical meeting that embellishes the story of Enoch, and the Bible speaks of Elijah (not Enoch) who is taken to heaven in a whirlwind as a chariot and horses of fire separated him from his companion Elisha (2 Kings 2:13). Clearly, symbolic language is used; unless we are to think of literal horses in the sky.

Holy scripture itself, however refers to an Enochian chariot exactly as it does to the "flashing sparks" (nonexistent!) which von Daniken "seems to remember" often surrounded the Ark of the Covenant (pp. 58-59). There were no flashing sparks, and no chariot is mentioned in the record of Enoch. This is a very disturbing, even distressing aspect about *Chariots of the Gods?* Its author "seems to remember," and very often hypothesizes, imaginative theories as though they were fact. In doing so, *Chariots* attacks that Book which is the treasured possession and guide to life for thousands upon thousands of people across the cultures of the world.

7

THOSE MAYAN MASTER-MINDS

Von Daniken seems overly credulous regarding the achievements of the Mayas of Central America. Their achievements were undoubtedly remarkable, but he clearly mixes folklore with established history.

The Mayan Popol Vuh

After telling us about Eskimo legends, which claim their first tribes were carried "by 'gods' with brazen wings," and of Red Indian sagas which mention a thunderbird introducing fire and fruit, von Daniken goes on:

Lastly, the Mayan legend, the Popol Vuh, tells us that the "gods" were able to recognize everything: the universe, the four cardinal points of the compass, and even the round shape of the earth (p. 75).

Clearly the extant version of the "Popol Vuh" contains a considerable amount of folklore — such as that about Zipacna, who killed 400 boys which then became the "Motz" group of stars(p. 101). It is said of Zipacna that "during the day he went about looking for food, and at night he carried mountains on his back" (p. 102).

It suits von Daniken to accept as authoritative the "Popol Vuh," which is traditionally accepted as a sacred book of the Mayas of Central America. It is believed that the "book" became known after the conquest of Mexico by the Spaniard Cortez, and was subsequently published in a Spanish form. However, the only copy today is in Latin. It is thought that the original would have been in pictographic form, somewhat resembling the Mexican codices — IF there were an original in writing. Some scholars advance this view (see *Sacred Books of the World*, A.C. Bouquet, p. 82). An original may have been destroyed at the time of the Conquest, but we wish to point out that it is not good scholarship to quote such a work as though it were definitely established as source material. This unwritten material is set forth concerning pre-historic times as though it were fully accredited as a text.

The Earth On a Crocodile

At this point let us consider the Mayan religion. Would von Daniken accept the Mayan belief that the earth rested on the back of a crocodile? (*Civilization Past and Present*, p. 597). Von Daniken insists — as shown above — that these people knew the earth was round. But how did the crocodile fit in? Perhaps there were enough of them to cover the four points of the compass.

As a matter of fact, knowledge of a round earth was not restricted to the Mayas. In the 2nd century B.C., Ptolemy represented the earth as a curved surface (*Civilization Past and Present*, p. 608). In the Christian Gospels we find that Jesus referred to His own return to earth in such a way as to indicate that the earth was round, i.e., two women would be grinding, other people would be working in fields, while others would be in bed. These activities were spread throughout the hours of the day and night, and hence required a round earth, for they were all taking place at the time, during the same event — His own return.

Another supposedly convincing fact quoted by von Daniken is that "the religious legends of the pre-Inca peoples say that the stars were inhabited and that the 'gods' came down to them from the constellation of the Pleiades" (p. 76). Do we also accept their belief that maize was the food of these gods who visited Central America? (*Civilization Past and Present*, p. 593).

The additional points are not irrelevant; they demonstrate that there is a great deal of demonstrably legendary material in the writings of these people. Von Daniken accepts as literal whatever suits his basic hypotheses.

A Limited Knowledge of the Mayas

Despite all the remarkable claims made for the Mayas, with their "incredible calculations" and inscriptions that "probably approach 400 million years" (p. 75), the fact is that:

> We probably know less about these South and Central American peoples than about any great civilization of the Old World. Most of our knowledge comes from archaeological research, recorded oral tradition, descriptions by early Spanish soldiers and priests, and the extraordinarily few surviving native records, such as three Mayan books of pictures and partially deciphered hieroglyphics (*Civilization Past and Present*, p. 595).

This authoritative statement comes from a recognized text, written by top American scholars associated with Universities such as Southern California and Stanford. The body of editors is impressive, and the publication date is 1969, the same year that von Daniken's book was published. However, the greater acceptance of experts and authorities does not necessarily mean that von Daniken is wrong. It is reasonable though, to ask that he substantiate his arguments, giving authorities where new information is submitted, and justifying dates and interpretations where these differ radically from those that are more traditionally accepted. Unfortunately, von Daniken does not conform to such standards, but makes many "new" statements that he simply does not substantiate.

To show how radically he disagrees with accepted scholarship we give one more brief quote from *Civilization Past and Present*.

> The Mayas developed a remarkably accurate calendar and a sophisticated writing system based on hieroglyphics, but aside from dates almost nothing has been deciphered . . . .

> After about 900 A.D. the Mayas of northern Guatemala appear to have abandoned their stately temple centers or cities — for reasons as yet unknown (p. 596).

The writer goes on to suggest a military invasion, and gives evidence of such activity with nearby peoples. Another possibility is also touched on in passing, for "disastrous droughts appear to have punctuated Mayan history . . . ."

These authors certainly do not suggest visits from spacemen which result in deserted sites. That sort of explanation is left to Erich von Daniken with his "we-know-better-than-the-scholars" approach.

Similarities To Other Religions

It is important to note that the Mayan religion had interesting similarities to the religions of

Babylonia, Assyria, and Egypt, as von Daniken himself suggests (p. 76). The Mayas had a tradition about a world-wide flood that destroyed mankind; they had gods of the sky, the earth, and the underworld; and human sacrifices were made to them. They had an amazing knowledge of astronomy, and even utilized observatories.

In these ways, they showed great similarities to other nations of antiquity, but this is not really surprising. Through the centuries men have been fascinated by the movements of heavenly bodies, and there are many known cases of their making careful calculations based on observations that have extended over long periods.

It is also thought-provoking to realize that these common traditions are somewhat similar to those in the first chapters of the Bible — up to the time of the confusion of man's language at Babel. There are archaeological writings in existence about these early incidents, and they are no longer regarded as quite unbelievable. If men WERE scattered at that time, as the Bible declares, it stands to reason that they would take those early stories — of creation, the flood, long-living men, and the confusion of languages — with them, and this in fact is the case. However, it is also true that though there are similarities to the Bible record there are also great differences. Many traditions have become distorted as they have been handed on across the world, while the Bible records are remarkably free of such corruption.

Calculations By An Electronic Brain?

Another absurd claim that von Daniken makes for the Mayas is that they possibly made calculations by means of an electronic brain (p. 76). This view is not held by archaeologists, but this does not especially concern von Daniken.

May we state here, however, that archaeologists do not credit these early Central Americans with established writing until about the 5th century A.D. Even if writing were known when their civilization is believed to have commenced (about a thousand years earlier), there is clearly no thought of such a people having the capacity for fantastic calculations and knowledge, such as astronomical details that supposedly could be accurately dated back to 27,000 years ago — as von Daniekn blithely tells us about these people.

Pyramids As Burial Sites

In other ways von Daniken leaves us confused in this section. Elsewhere he ridicules the possibility of a pyramid being "nothing more than the burial place of an extravagant king. Anyone who can believe that explanation is welcome to it . . ." (pp. 102-3). Now we learn of other huge pyramids which ARE the burial places of men after all. Or are they assembly places for the gods? (p. 120).

The Feathered Serpent

Von Daniken correctly associates the feathered serpent with the Mayas. One can see a connection with the serpent worshipped in Egypt and Canaan, and the serpent-like sirrush that appears so prolifically on the Ishtar Gate and Procession Way of ancient Babylon.

There are intersting theories about the Mayas and Aztecs bringing primitive religious ideas with them from Southeast Asia, but no one really knows. The similarity can as well be explained by the universal sameness of the nature of man, and by the existence of false gods willing to give some knowledge of spiritual realities, as long as the real truth was kept hidden.

However visits of gods in space chariots is another matter, one which demands a good imagination — it is credulity gone wild. What if we were to tell of that African legend of a woman who was pounding away at yams, when suddenly she raised her pole too high and it hit the sky-god 'Nyace in the face'. Who would believe it? But it is in fact a primitive African legend, and there are many more like it.

"Draunikou" In Fiji

Well do I remember one night in Figi, sitting entranced as I listened to legends and folklore of the Islands, I heard all about "draunikou" (a priest buries a piece of a man's hair, and soon that man dies): — it is rather like "pointing the bone" with the Australian aborigines. One interesting story concerned a man who forgot to throw a bowl of kava (the native drink) over the side of his fishing boat as an offering to the shark god. Later his child was born, and it had the face of a shark.

Interesting . . . fascinating . . . sometimes frightening — but should these legends be taken seriously as fact? Draunikou is a possibility of course, for there are psychological implications; but many other legends are not acceptable to reasoning people. After all, the shark-faced baby is never shown, and the legends of such people are not put down in writing until they themselves become "educated," long after the supposed incidents are no longer verifiable.

The Disappearance of the Mayan Civilization

Let us return to that mystery of the Mayan civilization which disappeared — according to the author of *Chariots* — about 600 A.D. (p. 121). I found myself bargaining for artefacts from the Mayan civilization on a recent trip to Latin America, and at the time undertook a little further research. Historians date the passing of this civilization at over 200 years later than the time given by von Daniken.

The conjecture is put forward in *Chariots* that because the Mayan civilization disappeared without trace, the people must have trekked far to the north. There they established another kingdom, with temples and pyramids erected according to the precise instructions of the gods — gods who had let the people down by not returning to the previous center, as expected! Von Daniken has this to say concerning his explanation of the disappearance of this civilization:

I should like to introduce a new note into the concert of opinions, a theory that is not proved any more than the other interpretations are. But regardless of the probability of the other explanations, I venture to make my contribution boldly and with conviction (p. 122).

We would not object to his making this unconfirmed speculation "boldly and with conviction" if it were not that he then presents his theories as though they were fact. Thus he presents a stone relief found in the region as a god, and says:

Our space traveller — he is clearly depicted as one . . . . The astronaut's front seat is separated by struts from the rear portion of the vehicle . . . (p. 124).

He states a hypothesis, then accepts it as fact. In philosophical terms, von Daniken is guilty of many non-sequiters. He makes jumps in his argument not justified by the evidence he presents. He jumps to conclusions which demand the acceptability of his earlier hypotheses, at times with little "proof" as to the valid connection between argument and conclusion.

Erich von Daniken states that various theories have been given to explain the sudden abandonment of this ancient center of culture, none of them convincing. However, this can be said about other sites as well. Trade routes change; earthquakes destroy thousands of people, while thousands of others leave through fear. Also, wars cause deportations of tens of thousands (witness the history of Israel and Judah), and even climatic changes can be pointed to as the cause of major shifts of population.

We do not always know the answer — as with the legendary Atlantis. Today it seems that Atlantis was more than legend, and there is serious thought that it lies buried beneath the sea.

Then, too, what about the mystery of the civilization at Bab-edh Dhra on the Moabite foothills? Apparently nobody visited there for about 600 years. We might say it is possible that this occurred because the inhabitants of Sodom and Gomorrah and the other "Cities of the Plain" had been wiped out. In general terms, the evidence from the ruins could fit the date of the Biblical incident.

Here, then, are two cases concerning the whereabouts of previous inhabitants. Neither is resolved by a space-gods theory, and neither has von Daniken built a convincing case for the Mayan civilization's disappearing because of the activity of space-gods. It is not an "either-or" case with spacemen as the favored alternative — even if it is an interesting conjecture.

Did the Civilization Disappear Entirely?

Erich von Daniken makes much of the supposed sudden disappearance of the Mayan civilization: so complete was this "absolutely incredible thing" that "no inhabitant ever returned there" (p. 121).

However, this is partially opposed to the facts. First, it is debatable that the civilization did disappear entirely. J. Eric S. Thompson, recognized as a leading authority in the field, suggests that a series of "peasants' revolts" occurred in which the rulers were killed, but that the peoples returned for religious purposes from time to time, even after the buildings had collapsed. He presents conclusive evidence, such as the presence of bodies, as well as every-day utensils like pottery and spindle-whorls, all clearly ABOVE the debris of the collapsed room (pp. 106-7).

Thompson suggests that "it is incorrect to suppose that this vast area had been a vacuum for hundreds of years" (p. 104). He proves his point by citing specific details of particular areas where settlements were known to have continued over the centuries. He tells of periodic visits to the actual religious sites themselves, and even of half-hearted attempts by the masons to keep the sites "in service" (p. 106).

All this clearly opposes von Daniken's sweeping assertion that "no inhabitant ever returned there." Interestingly enough, Thompson's views are a challenge to earlier archaeological opinion, which indicates that archaeologists are men of science, ready to face new alternatives as the case demands. This is different from the supposed dogmatism of archaeologists, to which we have already referred by quoting von Daniken.

That Astronaut Awaiting Blast-Off

In the center of *Chariots of the Gods?* is a series of pictures supposedly relating to space men who visited earth in days gone by. One of the pictures is of a figure resting in a Mayan Temple at Palenque in Mexico, which von Daniken likens "to a modern astronaut in his rocket."

This picture of the reclining figure has caused tremendous interest around the world, and as we conclude this chapter on the Mayas we wish to draw attention to a number of features as follows:

1. The "astronaut" has bare feet, and possibly no jacket.
2. He is wearing the usual Mayan shorts.

3. His head is outside the "rocket."

4. His "antenna" is nothing more than the usual Mayan hair-do.

5. A quetzal bird is perched on the top of the rocket — the national bird of Guatemala.

6. Serpents are depicted — also space-travellers?

7. The "rocket" is actually a throne, with its various components easily recognized.

8. Such thrones were used by both Mayas and dignitaries of neighboring countries for transport across the country by relays of slaves.

9. These dignitaries sat on the thrones at various angles, often reclining, as depicted by this figure, for they were carried like this for hours on end.

10. The inscription can be dated to A.D. 692, which does not coincide with von Daniken's projected single visit by astronauts, considerably earlier than this date.

The Mayas had a remarkable civilization, but as we study the facts we have no basis to take seriously von Daniken's hypotheses about astronauts who dropped in for a visit.

In fact, another Chariot has crashed. However, little damage was done. The reclining dignitary was moving at no more than five miles an hour anyway!

8

GODS OF THE NATIONS
AND THEIR
"BREEDING EXPERIMENTS"

In chapter 6 of *Chariots*, a virtual parade of deities comes forth as we are charioted swiftly from Eskimo mythology and Red Indian sagas to the Mayan ancestors of many of the people of Latin America. Chinese, African, Greek, and Roman writings and religious "treasures" are all brought in, as well as modern anti-religious activities in Germany, and many others.

Clearly, every aspect cannot be considered in this volume; but let us point out a few things which indicate the continuing approach of *Chariots*.

Hindu Gods and Chariots

One example in that chapter concerns Hindu religious writings. We learn concerning "this ancient Indian epic, the Mahabharata . . . even at a conservative estimate its original core is at least 5,000 years old" (pp. 76-77).

This might satisfy some readers, but it is certainly different from what A.C. Bouquet has to say in the volume to which I have previously referred:

The second great Indian epic, the "Mahabharata," may be compared to the "Iliad" of Homer, in that it is the account of a war between two armed alliances, the Pandavas and the Kurus (p. 227).

He goes on to say that its chief part is the famous "Gita," a didactic poem concerned with religious teaching. This is a comparatively late interpolation, and "as to date, it is placed by Radhakrishnan in the fifth century B.C." (p. 228).

H.D. Lewis and R.L. Slater suggest that the famous "Gita," part of "The Mahabharata," probably dates to the third or fourth century B.C. (at p. 41 in *The Study of Religions*). It appears to have been worked over in later centuries, possibly receiving both Buddhist and Christian influences (pp. 228,232).

In any case, von Daniken says that "the oldest books of mankind" came from Ur (p. 40), and then says that about 2,000 B.C. the Sumerians (from Ur) "began to record the glorious past of their people" (p. 40).Von Daniken is confusing when he talks of Indian writings "at least 5,000 years old," for he has also told us that oldest books of mankind date to 2,000 B.C. Are the Indian writings older than the Ur writings? Which dates do we accept?

Although the early sources of much Hindu writing are lost in antiquity, scholars are cautious about giving dates that stretch back too far. A core that is "at least 5,000 years old" — as quoted above from von Daniken — is questionable.

In passing, I notice another legend of a charioteer in the "Gita" itself. I read:

The scene is the great battlefield of Kurekshetra, the warrior is Arjuna, and the companion to whom he puts his questions is the god, Krisna, who is the high god Visnu, come to Arjuna's aid in the human guise of his charioteer (*The Study of Religions*, p. 38).

Here is yet another chariot of the gods, and so von Daniken tells us of another heavenly war chariot —

> And when Aryuna has found the gods after many perils, Indra, the lord of heaven, with his wife Sachi beside him, grants him a very exclusive audience. The two of them do not meet the valiant Aryuna just anywhere. They meet him in a heavenly war chariot and even invite him to travel in the sky with them (p. 78). (Note: Arjuna and Aryuna are alternate spellings.)

I find it hard to believe that von Daniken takes these legends and folklore so seriously. It seems clear that a great many such statements cannot possibly be taken as expressions of literal fact in the sense that von Daniken accepts them in *Chariots of the Gods?*

Another example from this same "Gita" in the "Mahabharata" is where Arjuna exclaims that Krisna is the god of gods, and Krisna replies in part:

> I am Visnu . . . I am Indra . . . I am Siva . . . I am the ocean . . . I am the Ganges River . . . I am the Ordainer (Creator) with faces in all directions . . . (*The Study of Religions*, p. 49).

Arjuna is then given a vision of this great god who has many mouths, eyes, arms, thighs, feet, bellies, and is "terrible with many tusks." Would this mean to von Daniken that this supreme Hindu deity is in fact an elephant?

Handwritings and the Bible Record
of Moses Rescued As a Child

Also in chapter 6, von Daniken tells of an Indian woman who put her child "in a little basket and put it in a river" (p. 78). He goes on to tell of a worthy man who fished the child out of the river and reared him. Then Erich von Daniken comments:

Really a story that is hardly worth mentioning if it were not so remarkably like the story of Moses! (p. 78).

If we accepted von Daniken's date — supposedly "conservative" — of 5,000 years for this "Mahabharata" in which the story appears, it implies that this incident occurred long before the time of Moses, and would therefore throw doubt on the credibility of the Bible story. However, we have seen that scholars accept a date of about the 3rd century B.C. for the Indian legend — about a thousand years AFTER Moses. We can assume, then, that this legend is borrowed from the Bible, and not the reverse.

The Egyptian God Ptah and his
"Gleaming Heavenly Chariot"

In the same chapter von Daniken mentions various Egyptian deities, and states:

The Egyptian pantheon is just as confusing. The ancient texts of the people on the Nile also tell of mighty beings who traversed the firmament in boats (p. 84).

He refers to a well-known text dedicated to the sungod Ra, telling of his drawing the ship of Aten (the sun disk) across the heavens. He quotes another inscription from one of the Pyramids which states it is Ra who "directs the sun ship of millions of years" (p. 84). These are supposedly chariots of the gods.

The god Ptah is singled out for special attention, he being the god Ra when he is actively associated

with the ancient Pharaonic city of Memphis. Again
I quote:

> Need I add that when the god Ptah came to
> give the king the models (celebrating the an-
> niversaries of his reign — Ed.) he appeared in
> a gleaming heavenly chariot and afterwards
> disappeared over the horizon in it. Today
> representations of the winged sun and a soar-
> ing falcon carrying the sign of eternity and
> eternal life can still be found on doors and
> temples at Edfu (p. 84).

We also learn in the same explanation that the
celebration was to take place for "six times a hundred thousand years."

The Creation of Egyptian Gods

According to *The Memphite Theology*, Ptah
created the other gods by thinking them into being.
Another Egyptian text states the creator sun-god
came from the waters of chaos — a development
associated with the functioning of eight strange
gods such as Darkness and Primeval Ocean. How
they can be earlier than the creator-god is not explained.

Other legends have the king participating in the
journeys of the sun. I.E.S. Edwards writes:

> Every day the king would accompany the
> sun-god on his voyage across the skies.
> Sometimes he is described as a rower in the
> barque . . . . Elsewhere he is promoted to the
> position of Captain of the barque (p. 33).

We could believe this sort of legend and religious
folklore as much as we could believe the literal
acceptance of von Daniken's "gleaming heavenly
chariot" for Ptah, to which I have referred. The
idea of the gods being associated with a heavenly
ship is a natural explanation of the recurring cycle
of day and night — as darkness comes, the gods of
the day are conquered by those of the night, but the

day gods will know a resurrection the next morning. Similar legends are associated with the gods of the Canaanites and various other peoples.

It is surprising to read of such "chariots" as boosters for the argument that the gods visited mankind, utilizing vehicles of this type.

Von Daniken Recognizes That Men "Became" Gods

The Egyptian belief that men "became" gods is also relevant in the hypotheses put forward by von Daniken. He recognizes this principle when he tells of the origin of Im-Hotep, the Egyptian god of medicine. I quote:

> The ground plan (of a building "of super-natural origin" — Ed.) was drawn by the deified being Im-Hotep. Now this Im-Hotep was a very mysterious and clever personality — the Einstein of his time. He was priest, scribe, doctor, architect, and philosopher rolled into one . . . the brilliant Im-Hotep built the step pyramid of Sakkara for his king, who was called Zoser . . . . The structure . . . was called the "House of eternity" by Im-Hotep. He had himself buried in it, so that the gods could wake him on their return (p. 85).

This is similar to the legends about the gods of Greece and Rome, but von Daniken puts forth something which is especially selected, such as "that the gods could wake him on their return." The gods have visited men — Im-Hotep awaits their return.

Von Daniken talks about the activities of these gods of Greece and Rome, especially in chapter 11 of *Gods From Outer Space*. He also discusses related concepts such as sex relations between gods and humans (e.g., at p. 147 of *Gods From Outer Space*), even when some of the gods were part animal (Ibid., page 147).

The following is relevant to gods of Greece and Rome, many of whom were originally great men of renown who ultimately became deified.

Men Who Became Gods

The Olympian gods of Greece supposedly were concerned intimately with mankind, ready to help and encourage that which was good and to banish that which was foolish. As I have said, the gods developed from real men possessed of vast power and energy; but when they "became gods, it was at the same time recognized that they were imperfect and finite. Though possessed of great strength, they were not almighty, and though "deathless" they were not in the true sense eternal. They were different from the astral gods, such as Helios the sun god and Selene the moon goddess, who moved in their own courses and were virtually indifferent to the affairs of men.

In the Homeric age, each deity was thought to have a separate house, magnificently designed and furnished. If the gods came like bolts of lightning from the sky there would be worthy houses for them — thus Zeus had his temple at Olympia, Athene had the Parthenon in Athens, while Apollo could reside at Delphi — and each had other smaller houses in different places. The good god Hermes and the bad god Ares had smaller houses because each was thought to be always on the move.

A God Who Swallowed His Children

Zeus was the god of the sky and the weather. About 600 B.C., he was conceived by the Greeks to be either the sky itself or the great being that lived in the sky, and so was responsible for the weather. He was supposed to live on the summit of Mt. Olympus, the highest point in Greece. But where did he come from?

The Greeks explained how their "creator" god, Zeus came into being. The god Kronos swallowed all his own children by the goddess Rhea (his own sister), except for his youngest child Zeus — he swallowed a stone instead of this child. Zeus was then hidden in a cave in Crete, tended by animals, and protected by armed spirits. Zeus soon forced Kronos to vomit forth his brothers and sisters, and a great "battle of the gods and giants" took place. Then began Zeus' visits to men and women.

How different all this is from the majestic concept of Jehovah, whose character is presented in the Judeo-Christian record!

The Greek idea was to worship a god through his representation in a statue; in this way he was praising that god. In a sense, this is anthropomorphic religion wherein gods are represented in human form. The Greeks maintained the concept that the athlete was the nearest humans came to physical perfection, and so was nearest to their gods. This was tied to their "humanism," for to them gods were ideal human beings.

Thus they thought of Zeus as a divine athlete, and as such he was presented naked, inasmuch as it became the practice for athletes to run unclothed. Zeus was the prototype of mankind, created as a perfect image of man. Thus the poet Homer did not look on men as created in the image of God, but rather he looked on gods as made in the likeness of men.

The Human Body "Deified"

Zeus as the "creator" who loved mankind had to be depicted as an ideal man, physically perfect. This "worship" of the human body is seen in the very manner of Greek dating. Christians date their calendar from the "Year of our Lord," and the Romans from the foundation of Rome, but the ancient Greeks thought in terms of the first Olympiad,

776 B.C. An Olympiad was the period of four years between one religio-athletic festival and the next, held at Olympia.

Referring to this new approach to athletic prowess Charles Seltman says:

The institution of organized athletics as an act of worship toward Zeus, and of the body trained to perfection as a thing dedicated to God, was a new and most startling concept in the history of mankind. But it was the necessary prelude to the birth of humanism (*The Twelve Olympians*, p. 40).

Gods Begetting Man

The aforementioned material is background to another von Daniken hypothesis on the relationship between gods and mankind.

We have referred to his statements on the various gods in chapter 6 of *Chariots of the Gods?* In that chapter (and in other places) he refers to the fertilization of humans by gods:

And, of course, there is yet another reference to the fertilization of humans by gods. Like Gilgamesh, Aryuna, the hero of the Mahabharata, undertakes a long journey in order to seek the gods and ask them for weapons . . . (p. 78).

Here we have another "special" interpretation, a weaving together of a fabric of fact and fiction, of figures and symbols. They are all presented authoritatively, as though no other interpretation were possible. If he did not use illustrations from the Bible, we would ignore the argument — and other points of his discussion. However, because Christians, Jews and other have been offended, and even confused, by the "evidence" he presents, we offer a reply. We refer especially to his comment concerning "the fertilization of humans by gods."

Some of von Daniken's statements on this subject follow, with our comments:

The gods of the dim past have left countless traces which we can read and decipher today for the first time . . . . space travel, so topical today, was not a problem, but a reality, to the men of thousands of years ago (p.11).

A wild theory becomes fact! The "problem" is resolved, we "read" the traces left behind by the gods, and space travel was a "reality" to men thousands of years ago. It is all so definite; von Daniken continues to give us his insufficiently explained hypotheses as fact, then moves to unsubstantiated conclusions.

Even though I do not yet know who these extra-terrestrial intelligences were or from which planet they came, I nevertheless proclaim that these 'strangers' annihilated part of mankind existing at the time and produced a new, perhaps the first, homo sapiens (p. 12).

The author acknowledges he does not know who they were or where they came from — yet if they have left those "countless traces" which "we can read and decipher today," why does he have to make such an admission?

Even when facing the dearth of evidence, von Daniken is not short of ideas. At page 76 he tells us that some of the gods came "from the constellation of the Pleiades," while at pages 154 and 155 he speculates as to Martian visitors.

Where von Daniken's Homo Sapiens Came From

It is also difficult to understand something else about von Daniken's god-men, his supposed first *homo sapiens*. At page 155 he takes his conjecture a step further, as he suggests the possibility that his space visitors actually came from Mars — again establishing *homo sapiens* by interbreeding "with the semi-intelligent beings living there''.

Then comes perhaps the strangest part. These new men, these giants who were god-men, "finally died out" (p. 155). Surely this would not be the fate of such a super-race? We would expect the weaker, earth-bound mortals to die out — but perhaps that would involve finding these god-men today, and unfortunately that is not so easy!

Von Daniken also has these "giants who come from the stars" moving "enormous blocks of stone," but we know from written records and other evidence that the Pyramids and those huge statues at Easter Island did not require the help of giants. Thus another chariot goes crashing in flames, carrying his giant astronaut-breeder-builder into the abyss of unsupported theories.

Chariots of the Gods? is a strange book. On page 58 we have radio beams which originate from intelligent beings in space. In that context von Daniken says:

> This realization could mean a kind of coup de grace to the search for other living beings on the universe.

We were told of gods' visiting us from outer space, and that these visitors interbred with mankind. Where do his contradictions end?

In challenging Christian beliefs, von Daniken asks if "a single Christian" would be prepared "to recognize the god of the pre-Inca culture as the GENUINE god because of the excavations in Peru" (p. 73). We trust the answer is "No!" for the evidence certainly does NOT warrant such a drastic conversion. However, let us tie this also to von Daniken's proclamation that gods came to earth and influenced future life:

> The religious legends of the pre-Inca peoples say that the stars were inhabited and that the

"gods" came down to them from the constellation of the Pleiades . . . and promised immortality to individual men . . . (p. 76).

Gods Conduct Several Breeding Experiments With Humans

This promise of immortality is linked with fertilization by the gods, for von Daniken ties it in with the Epic of Gilgamesh which includes the Babylonian story of the Flood:

We learn that Gilgamesh was a mixture of "god" and man — two-thirds "god," one-third man. Pilgrims who came to Uruk gazed up at him in fear and trembling because they had never seen his like for beauty and strength. In other words, the beginning of the narrative contains the idea of inter-breeding between "god" and man yet again (p. 64).

According to von Daniken's theory, too, "it needed several experiments before men finally turned out as successfully as 'God' wanted" (p. 62). Another contradiction follows, as the author states, "We could postulate that today we are similarly constituted to those fabulous unidentified beings." Yet he has stated that the race "finally died out" (see above), though they were supposed to be *homo sapiens*, the name for man today.

Contradictions and confusion — where will they end? Von Daniken's book is disturbing, for many people have taken it seriously. When discussing the credence some people give his theories, it is relevant to discuss von Daniken's interpretation as applied to the Bible at this point. This present writing of an "alternative" to the *Chariots* is not only meant for the Christian reader.

It is difficult to explain why the Bible cannot be read and understood by everyone in the way that an "ordinary" book can be understood. Spiritual writings demand spiritual language and spiritual understanding. The Bible is self-consistent as it presents doctrine and theology, but this self-consistency is not always readily apparent. Somewhat the same attitude must be taken with other "spiritual" writings. A knowledge of the particular religion or philosophy makes the writing much more understandable.

It almost seems that God demands a point of faith before one can appreciate the marvels of His Book. Many people approach it with cynicism, or with a swaggering, critical attitude that implies that God is fortunate to have such a person showing ANY interest. To such persons, the Book's treasures are simply not discovered; for this Book of Spiritual Values demands spiritual understanding. In fact, it calls for re-birth by the Spirit of God Who — according to the Bible itself — is the ultimate Divine Author.

What the Bible Says About Sons of God

For the Christian and Jew, the claims presented by von Daniken, that gods fertilized human stock with Divine seed are offensive, as well as being based on unacceptable exegesis. On page 51 he asks, "Where do the 'sons of God' come from?", then goes on to quote Genesis 6:4 as to there being giants in the earth in those early days. He next states:

Once again we have the sons of God, who interbreed with human beings. Here, too, we have the first mention of giants . . . . What sort of creatures were they, these "giants?" Were they our forefathers, who built the gigantic buildings and effortlessly manhandled the monoliths, or were they technically skilled space travellers from another star?

Let us examine the Bible at this point. First, these "giants" are introduced literally thousands of years after Adam, who, the Bible states, was the first man. The word "giant" is used again in ordinary narrative parts of Scripture — one example is shown at Numbers 13:33, where it does not refer to a breed who were part-god and part-human.

According to the Bible, two lines had developed in the history of man by the time of that statement about "the sons of God" in Genesis, chapter 6. These were the Godly line of Seth and the ungodly line of Cain, who killed his brother Abel, and went into "exile." The first human baby, according to the Bible, became a murderer.

Many Biblical scholars accept that "the sons of God" were the line of Seth and that a measure of intermarriage took place with "the daughters of men," the ungodly line of Cain. The statement "there were giants in the earth in those days" is simply a factual presentation, an example of other facts in this abbreviated history of mankind's early days.

Were these giants "angels?" Jesus said that angels are without sex (at Matthew 22:30), and that when men enter into eternal life beyond this life they do not marry.

Other scholars believe that "the sons of God" were fallen angels who now co-habited with "the daughters of men" and that giants were the result of this union. However, "took them wives" was the normal term for marriage, and did not refer to a casual sex relationship. Also, "giant" is not always used in a special way: it may mean "giant" as we would think of it in modern times (giants have been relatively common in all ages). The Hebrew record does not imply a casual relationship between the sexual union and giants; therefore, there is no compelling argument showing that this relationship is linked to the statement about the birth of giants. "There were giants in the earth" at Genesis 6:4 is a later statement than that of the sex union at verse 2, and the two statements are not necessarily casually related.

In any case, the Bible teaching is different from that of von Daniken, who wants us to believe *homo sapiens* were taken off to another planet, and were subjected to repeated breeding experiments, with any unfortunate results destroyed (pp. 71-72). According to this theory on the earth itself:

A few specially selected women would be fertilized by the astronauts. Thus a new race would arise that skipped a stage in natural evolution (p. 25).

Robert L. Whitelaw, Professor of Mechanical Engineering at the Virginia Polytechnic Institute wrote a booklet which presents data from 15,000 radiocarbon dates. He states at pages 3-4:

With this method which was invented by Dr. Libby around 1947, and for which he received the Nobel Prize, it has now been possible by the concerted action of some 91 universities and laboratories from many countries to accumulate over 15,000 dates of once-living matter gathered all over the face of the earth. Practically nothing has been left untouched in this vast endeavor. This method, called radiocarbon dating, only gives the death-date of once living things. Also, because it uses an isotope that has a half life of 5,570 years, it can only detect death-dates that lie within 6 or 7 times that value. Anything older would show up as an . . . undatable specimen.

Millions of Years Shrink to Recent Times After All

The first amazing thing that comes out of surveying all these dates, which by the way, are available to everyone of you in the annual journal "Radiocarbon," is that everything they have picked up, with practically no exception whatsoever, has proved to be datable. In the list of specimens they have dated we find practically all the fossils and ancient men that were supposed to be back in the millions of years of age. Here is just a partial list I have compiled from over 220 specimens identified as fossils. These are 220 out of over 15,-000. For instance, here is the Neanderthal man — 32,000 years; here is the sabre-tooth tiger taken out of the enormous fossil community of bones in the La Brea Tar Pits in Los Angeles — 28,000 years; here is coal supposedly in the carboniferous period of 200 to 300 million years ago dated as 1,680 years. Here is a fossil tree dated in Russia — 11,700 years. Here is one of the supposedly prehistoric men; Rhodesia man or "Broken-Hill" man as he is called — 9,000 years. Here is another Neanderthal — 40,000 years; here is petrified wood — 10,000 years; here is an entire collection of prehistoric, now extinct, animals found near Evansville, Indiana — 9,400 years; here are Mastodon bones found at Thamesville and Chatham, Ontario, dated at 8,900 years. Even crude oil, which again is supposed to be carboniferous has been dated in California and natural gas in Mississippi. Finally, in view of the recent publicity given to the work of Dr. Leakey in the Olduvai Gorge in Africa in which a "hominid" skull was reported to be 2 to 4 million years of age, mammal bones at the same site and depth have now been dated and published in this year's volume — 10,100 years. Even the findings still more recently reported, in the September 20, 1969, issue of *NATURE* to be older than Leakey's, found in the Omo Valley of Ethiopia, are now dated in Radiocarbon at 15,500 years.

In the light of this kind of evidence, some scientists are frankly admitting there must be a serious re-appraisal of the whole geological scale of dating and of other practices in paleontology as well. Most, however, are apparently ignoring these dates in the hope that radiocarbon may not be so accurate after all.

The true God HAS come to earth — in the Person of His Son Jesus Christ. Men ARE taken to a realm beyond the earth, but not in a space ship or in bodies that need special helmets to prevent destruction by fire. Jesus Christ offers eternal life, and when that life is finally assumed in its fullness, this corruptible must put on incorruption, this mortal must put on immortality (I Corinthians 15:53).

That is the Christian hope, to be realized when Jesus Christ the Son of God returns. His promise is repeated at the very end of the Holy Bible, with the appropriate response of the Christian,

"Even so, come, Lord Jesus" (Rev. 22:20).

9

LIFE ON OTHER PLANETS?

Clifford Wilson Talks
To a Physicist About "Chariots"

A Dialogue with Dr. Frederick H. Giles, Jr.,
Associate Professor, Department of Physics
and Astronomy, University of South Carolina,
Columbia, S.C., U.S.A.

(Dr. Giles has passed away since this interview took place. Except for minor editing it is
reprinted without alteration.)

WILSON: In his book *Chariots of the Gods?* Erich
von Daniken writes at length about other planetary
systems. Can you explain why it is conjectured that
there are other systems besides the one which includes the earth?

GILES: One point often advanced is that our sun is
itself a star similar to many others, so why would
there not be other planetary systems?

How Would Planets Originate?

WILSON: If there were such systems, how would their origin be explained?

GILES: If planets came into being during the life history of particular stars, there is a feasible explanation. Some of the younger stars seem to be rotating relatively rapidly when compared with stars which are a little older, and there appears to be rather an abrupt change in the rotating characteristics of these older stars as compared with the younger — a change that apparently takes place a particular age point.

WILSON: So what is the conjecture — how is this changed rotating characteristic related to the formation of planets?

GILES: One possibility is that as stars grow older and pass through this particular age point, they tend to throw off planets; and that the extra spin of the younger stars is then taken up by the new planet or planets which are moving around the star. Thus, according to this theory, the star itself would rotate less rapidly.

WILSON: So this theory would explain why the star at a certain age appears to rotate less rapidly; but are any of those supposed new planets visible?

GILES: It would be virtually impossible to see such planets as we see stars. They are essentially invisible — they do not emit light of themselves, and they would be very small relative to the size of the star around which they would revolve.

WILSON: So these "planets" would not be other stars, but smaller throw-offs?

GILES: They would be more in the nature of a satellite, not other stars or planets really; another name is "dark companion" or "dark binary." Such a "dark companion" could even be a great piece of rock.

What Evidence Of Other Planets?

WILSON: You have said it would be impossible to see such a "dark companion", but I gather its presence could be indicated by the changed rotating characteristic of a star — would you elaborate?

GILES: The theory is that if there were such a dark companion, its presence would be indicated by an irregular wobble in the star itself as the planet revolved around it, such as there is a wobble of the earth as the moon goes around it every 30 days.

WILSON: Is there any direct evidence that there ARE other planetary systems?

GILES: No. There is one other case where the inference from the "wobble" points to another planet — this exception is known as "Barnard's Star." This star has a measurable wobble — the wobble is very slight, but it is measurable. This could indicate that there is a dark companion to this star, a satellite.

WILSON: Would the distances involved make the detection of such wobbles difficult?

GILES: Yes. Even the nearest star is supposedly four light years away, and the detection of a wobble is very difficult. If we accept that light travels at 186,000 miles per second, and that the nearest star is four light years away, it becomes clear that theories about other planets are highly conjectural.

WILSON: You have already said that it is only conjecture that there are other planetary systems. What about life on von Daniken's conjectured planets — is that possible?

GILES: Von Daniken begins with the arguments of Harlow Shapley, who was a Harvard astronomer. Shapley was one of the early astronomers of modern times, who became convinced that man is too apt to see himself as the center of all things, and he writes belittling man's place. He stresses that our system is not even at the center of the galaxy.

Shapley's conjectures are by no means universally accepted by astro-physicists; and, in fact, they have been widely challenged. However, his arguments are in a very different category from those of von Daniken in *Chariots of the Gods?*, exemplified by this statement from *Chariots*:

> There is no doubt about the existence of planets similar to the earth — with a similar mixture of atmospheric gases, similar gravity, similar flora and possibly even similar fauna (p. 17).

All this is based on Shapley's writings, but it jumps rapidly from a legitimate (though controversial) conjecture to "There is no doubt."

No Secret Conference!

WILSON: On page 165 of *Chariots*, the author refers to a "secret conference" that took place in November, 1961, in the National Radio Astronomy Observatory at Green Bank in West Virginia. You have shown me a copy of a report of this conference. Would you care to comment?

GILES: It was not a "secret conference," and the report is openly published.

WILSON: I see it emanates from the Goddard Space-Flight Center, NASA. Do its propositions agree with those of von Daniken?

GILES: Not at all. Let me give you a typical quote from just one page:

> Estimation of the fraction of stars which form planets is subject to great uncertainty and, although several different arguments may be adduced, they are all weak . . . .
> Estimation of the average number of planets per system with environments suitable for the development of life, is a matter of pure guesswork. Mass, composition, temperature, and many other factors are important. Little

as we know of the probability of occurrence of
planetary systems, we know nothing of the
details of any other planetary system but our
own (J.P.T. Pearman, p. 289 in *Ex-
traterrestrial Intelligent Life and
Interstellar Communication: An Infor-
mal Discussion*).

"There Is No Doubt" — Or
"Pure Guesswork?"

This conference discussed the probability of intelligent life on other planets, but the point should
be made very strongly that the whole approach was
diametrically opposed to von Daniken's statement
that "there is no doubt" as to the existence of other
planets. This conference openly stated that such a
conjecture was a matter of "pure guesswork."

WILSON: Could you outline briefly what you see as
the problems associated with intelligent life on
other planets?

GILES: We have already seen that the first
problem is, "Are there other planets anyway?"
Then if there is even one such planet, will it have
the right conditions for the maintaining of life, such
conditions as the right temperature range? For example, if the temperature is too high, the complexity of the chemical processes is such that they simply do not hold together. If the temperature is too
low, the chemical processes do not occur rapidly
enough for living things to arrive at a point of
change; and therefore even the process of thinking
would be out of the question. So it follows that if we
are thinking of a form of life that involves
chemistry, the temperature range is very important.

There are other problems: such a planet must be
commodious; it must not be too heavy, or it would
plaster life to its earth; it must not be too light, for

some sort of atmosphere would need to be maintained. Then, too, the planet must be the right distance from the star from which it originally spun off. There would need to be a long time span for a self-replicating system to emerge. If we did accept the theory that life on this planet is between 2 and 5 billion years old, this would not give any assurance of the development of life anywhere else. And we might also ask "How much time have we got to allow for such development?"

WILSON: You talk about "life" — do you mean intelligent life that existed billions of years ago?

GILES: No — just "life." The emergence of sentient, conscious, intelligent life involves further problems. If all the other conditions were met (all the problems we have already discussed), we would still need enough time for the complexity of intelligent life to appear. Then, even if there were intelligent beings, that does not mean that their technology would be highly developed. It would be an exceedingly complex operation for them to communicate with beings on earth or any other planet — even if they had the tremendous periods of time necessary for such an operation.

If we accepted that, at a conservative estimate, it would take four light years for such a signal to be sent and received on earth, presumably it would take four more light years for the return signal. By that time, the original operators would have been long since dead.

Von Daniken's Unsupportable Theories

WILSON: Am I right in concluding that von Daniken's hypotheses are not supported by facts?

GILES: Yes — the points I have made are only some of the ways in which von Daniken's hypothesis is quite unacceptable. His arguments are interesting, but not really supportable. If we apply our minds to it, we can arrive at any kind of theory; but the question is whether it is supported by facts, or whether it is science fiction.

I recently came across an article by Martin Gardner in *The Scientific American* which bears on this point. Gardner points out that since the beginning of history "unusual coincidences have strengthened belief in the influence on life of occult forces."

Relating this to von Daniken's book, in this case, it appears that "unusual coincidences have strengthened belief in the influence on life" of non-terrestrial intelligent beings. It is possible to take disconnected facts from the mass of material available and make a seemingly connected presentation, and this is what von Daniken has done. He has picked up some of the most conjectural areas of physics and astronomy, and selected his own array of quite unconnected facts or suppositions, then built on them as though they were established and connected facts.

In the article, Martin Gardner quotes G.K. Chesterton: "Life is full of a ceaseless shower of small coincidences . . . . It is this that lends a frightful plausibility to all false doctrines and evil fads. There are always such props of accidental arguments upon anything."

WILSON: Would you state once more that basis for the conjecture that there is life on other planets?

GILES: The only planet that we know for sure has life on it is the earth. One other star has been detected with a slight wobble, and this could mean that it has an invisible dark companion moving around it. Such a dark companion would make the star itself wobble. As a very slight wobble has been measured in relation to one star, some astronomers conjecture that the wobble is caused by a planet rotating around the star.

Von Daniken's Lack of Scientific Precision

WILSON: That seems rather flimsy evidence for von Daniken's statement that undoubtedly there are other planets similar to the earth!

GILES: What you say is right. Even if astronomers calculate in terms of probability for such bodies — and some do — they never use the terms of certainty which von Daniken does. His hypotheses simply do not fit the facts, but that is typical of his approach at many places. He has not the precision expected of scientific writing.

WILSON: Could you give another example?

GILES: Well, on page 158 he writes about the exact measurement of about 10 milliard light years. Then on page 159 he seems to be suggesting that laser light beams travel faster than radio — his wording is somewhat ambiguous, but the fact is that laser light travels no faster than radio waves.

Von Daniken's whole approach is open to question, and his interpretations are often distorted. One example is where he suggests that physicists at Princeton made a certain discovery relating to elementary particles, and that this new discovery was theoretically impossible.

The physicists would deny that emphatically. They would agree that what they observed did not fit the currently accepted theory, but this may be the fault of the initial interpretation, or the theory might not have been sufficiently comprehensive to handle the new situation. If so, the theory would need to be changed, or modified, or expanded, to accommodate the new facts, and the physicists would be the first to admit it.

In this particular case a number of experiments have been carried out to see what revision should be made to the theory. Checks are made to determine whether the experiment was poorly done, or whether there was an initial error, or even to find out if possibly the theory is adequate. If this last is true, there are exciting new possibilities.

A Final Comment

WILSON: What is your final comment about von Daniken's book, *Chariots of the Gods?*

GILES: He takes conjectures, accepts them as facts, builds way-out theories on them, and presents his "many small coincidences" according to his own preconceived notions. He deliberately chooses the unconnected, weaves a semblance of connection around it, and presents his theories as foregone conclusions. This approach is often used by writers; it may make exciting reading, but one dare not accept it as substantially credible.

10

PUTTING THE RECORD STRAIGHT
ABOUT ARCHAEOLOGY AND
THE BIBLE

Von Daniken appears to have a bias against archaeology, as we have pointed out. In fact, it was because of this that a number of people urged me to write this survey. He refers to the evidence from archaeology verifying facts in the Old Testament, then states that such verified facts are not proof as to the religion itself. He argues that such finds merely show that people lived in a particular area, but "they do not prove that the God of that people was the one and only god (and not a space traveler)" (p. 73).

In another of my booklets, *Archaeology and the Bible Student*, I make four specific points regarding the relevance of archaeology for the Bible student. These are summarized on the first two pages of that booklet as follows:

(a) Archaeology has confirmed the accuracy of many Bible incidents and stories;

(b) Archaeology shows that many customs of ancient peoples are recorded in the Scriptures;

(c) Archaeology has added to our knowledge of peoples and lands of the Bible; and

(d) Archaeology has endorsed the meaning of many words and phrases which previously were unknown.

Numerous other examples are given, and this adds up to a convincing presentation of the claim that the Bible is the world's most remarkably accurate history textbook. It also demonstrates that the Old Testament writings were written against the backgrounds claimed for them. We have referred to Messianic prophecies, those remarkable Old Testament pre-writings which the Christian sees fulfilled in Jesus Christ. Their genuineness is attested in various ways, not the least being that the men who wrote such accurate history (as archaeological research demonstrates) also wrote those prophecies. This becomes a telling argument that conveys a forceful challenge to accept the spiritual message of the Bible, God's Word of Truth.

We do not need to argue that "archaeology proves the Bible." The Bible is quite able to vindicate itself. Someone has said that it is like a lion: let it loose and it looks after itself.

This is also the Book that gives us the knowledge of God in Jesus Christ, and it is well said that the closer one draws to this Book, the closer one draws to God, and to his fellow-man.

According to the Bible (e.g., at John 14:6, Acts 4:12), it is not true that all religions are one, or that it matters little by what name we worship God. The Bible makes it clear that God is a jealous God, not to be equated with Baal or any other false god of the surrounding nations.

We have demonstrated that there are opposing evil powers, and von Daniken himself recognizes the widespread nature of this belief. He links the serpent with evil as he states:

Primeval image of evil, the snake is condemned to crawl. How could anyone worship this repulsive creature as a god and why could it fly into the bargain? Among the Mayas it could (p. 127).

It is indeed strange, yet again the original source can be traced to the record at Genesis, chapter 3. It is interesting to compare those early chapters of Genesis with the Sumerian *Epic of Emmerkar* which tells of the "pure" land of Dilmun where "the lion killed not, the wolf snatched not the lamb" (S.H. Hooke, *Middle Eastern Mythology*, p. 114). Once again, we can see the uncorrupted original in the Bible record of the Garden of Eden.

Even the author of *Chariots* acknowledges the presence of evil powers. The Bible clearly teaches that the leader of these powers is Satan, and that at times he masquerades as an angel of light. He is quite willing for individual men and women to have some INTELLECTUAL perception of God, as long as they do not come to SPIRITUAL perception as well, and grasp the true reality.

Thus, as we study various ideas about the gods prevalent among the nations, we see an occasional gleam of light.

Archaeology demonstrates the existence of people who, the Bible claims, lived long ago. Not too long ago it was thought that the Hittite people were not known in the days of Abraham, then thousands of their clay tablets were found and it was shown that there was a branch of the Hittites this early — as the Bible indicates in Genesis, chapter 23.

Archaeology does not only inform us about people who lived long ago, but also about many of the places mentioned in Scripture. In I Kings 10:28, reference is made to a place called Kue. At one time, scholars thought this should be translated to mean "linen yarn," because of a similar Hebrew word; but now we know that it was an actual place, a place famous for its horses. This exactly fits the context of that verse in I Kings 10:23 where we read of Solomon buying horses from Egypt — "and from Que." We now know that "Que" was the ancient name for Cilicia, famous for its white horses. One horse from Que was worth four from Egypt — Solomon bought the best! Thus the Bible verse should read that Solomon bought horses from Egypt and from Que, and not that Solomon bought horses from Egypt "and linen yarn." Archaeology has resolved this particular linguistic problem.

In the 1800's the German scholar Julius Wellhausen wrote,

> It is true that we attain to no historical knowledge of the Patriarchs, but only of the time when the stories about them arose in the Israelite people . . . . this later age is here unconsciously projected in its inner and outward features into hoary antiquity, and is reflected there like a glorified image, *History of Israel*, English translation, 1885).

Contrast the above with modern knowledge based on archaeological evidence, and we find many refreshing scholarly assessments, such as this statement from Professor W.F. Albright:

> So many corroborations of detail have been discovered in recent years that most competent scholars have given up the old critical theory according to which the stories of the Patriarchs are mostly retrojections from the time of the dual monarchy, 9th-8th centuries B.C. (p. 183, *From Stone Age to Christianity*).

The old idea was that the stories of the Patriarchs grew with the telling and were not committed to writing for many centuries. Now a new respect has come for the early Bible records, for the evidence from clay tablets assures us that the source documents of Genesis give remarkable details about ancient customs. Many of those customs had become unknown by the time of the divided kingdom following Solomon's death — the old idea of the Documentary Hypothesis was that they were put in writing after the time of Solomon.

It is much easier to accept that the stories of Abraham were put in writing in his time than that they knew the embellishments of centuries of re-telling, yet at the same time retained ancient customs which were no longer understood by the later listeners!

Customs and local color are remarkably accurate throughout the Scriptures. For instance, in 2 Kings 15:19,20 we read that the Israelite King Menahem had to pay 50 shekels tribute for the men of Israel, for this was demanded by the Assyrians who were besieging him. Tablets excavated from the Assyrian city of Nimrud show that at that time the current price of an able-bodied slave was 50 shekels of silver. It seems that King Menahem had the option of either paying the price for his men to be redeemed from slavery or for them to be taken into captivity — as they were within less than a generation. The 50 shekels is seen in a much clearer light when we understand that this was the current price of a slave.

Scriptural writers also used local color in the correct use of titles. Bible writers confidently use titles of people around them, and they use them accurately; they were eye-witnesses of the things about which they wrote. Thus various titles — such as "house overseer" (Gen. 39:4) — are correctly used in the Joseph narrative. The titles given to Joseph and the description of his investiture (Gen. 41:39-45; 45:8) are paralleled in Egyptian tomb paintings.

During the times of the Assyrians we find titles such as Tartan (Commander-in-Chief), Rabshakeh (Chief of the Princes), and Rabsaris (Chief Eunuch) used correctly, each of these three being found in 2 Kings 18:17. These and several other official titles were correctly used by Bible writers who obviously were in direct contact with Assyrian people, for the Assyrians disappeared as a people in 605 B.C., never to be known again.

Someone might say, however: "Well, there are still Syrians today." The Syrians are a different people. The Assyrians and the Syrians lived in neighboring areas, but they were not the same people. Bible writers who used Assyrian titles were contemporary onlookers.

One might try this with the titles of our own army, navy, or air force, and then extend it to neighboring peoples. Mistakes do creep in — for instance, an Australian Army Captain is lower in rank compared with a Captain in the Royal Australian Navy.

One can extend this test to the last dozen or so kings or rulers of a particular country, then to a neighboring country. Few can do this accurately (as experiments at lectures over years have shown!) yet Bible writers use their own titles, and the titles of their enemies. They list their own kings, and very often they tell us who the opposing kings are, always in proper chronological sequence.

This is clear evidence of genuineness, and the numbers of similar confirmations from the times of Solomon to the collapse of the Assyrian Empire are simply staggering.

These Assyrian people disappeared 600 years before Christ, and we have a remarkable argument as to the genuineness of many prophecies by those same writers as they accurately foresaw the Person and work of Jesus Christ. The Bible itself says, "Holy men of God spoke as they were moved by the Holy Spirit" (2 Peter 1:21).

In the years following Solomon, several kings of Israel and Judah are known from archaeological evidence. The Assyrian King Shalmaneser III recorded the part that Ahab, King of Israel, played in the Battle of Karkar (853 B.C.); the same Shalmaneser referred to tribute paid by "Jehu, son of Omri" (841 B.C.) — thus referring to two kings of Israel in the one context. The Assyrian king Tiglath Pileser refers to both Menahem (738 B.C.) and Pekah (about 734 B.C.), and Sennacherib refers to "Hezekiah the Jew" (701 B.C.).

An Old-Time Murder

The murder of the Assyrian King Sennacherib is recorded in the Bible (2 Kings 19) and we find the same story told in clay tablets from the annals of King Esarhaddon who succeeded Sennacherib (2 Kings 19:37). The story is taken even further in the records of Ashurbanipal who succeeded Esarhaddon — he had the King's assassins killed in the temple where they had committed the crime. Both Esarhaddon and Ashurbanipal confirm that Sennacherib was killed by his own sons.

Other Bible kings are referred to in the Assyrian period, as when Esarhaddon mentions Manasseh (about 675 B.C.). The accurate listing of kings and rulers is not limited to the Old Testament. Herod the Great, Archelaus, Agrippa, and Festus are but four of the rulers correctly identified in the New Testament.

When one examines the Bible and other records of

the time, one can see they are indeed contemporary. The source documents of Scripture are dated consistently with the time implicit in their own claims.

Most Bible students know that the Babylonian King Nebuchadnezzar besieged the Judeans and eventually destroyed Jerusalem in 587 B.C. His own records have presented details of his Palestine campaigns, again endorsing the facts given in the records of Scripture.

In Daniel 4:30, we read of King Nebuchadnezzar's boast about the magnificent city of Babylon: "Is not this great Babylon, that I have built for the house of the kingdom by the might of my power, and for the honor of my majesty?"

Babylon was glorious among ancient cities, but the knowledge that Nebuchadnezzar had largely rebuilt it was lost to secular scholarship until Professor Koldewey of Germany excavated it from 1899 to 1914. Nebuchadnezzar boasted of his great achievements on stamped bricks, cylinders of clay, and various other building inscriptions. The statement above, from Daniel 4:30, is the sort of inscription that the boastful Nebuchadnezzar would have written.

But how did Daniel know it was King Nebuchadnezzar who rebuilt Babylon, when other historians had forgotten? Daniel knew, for he was there as a captive. This is the story given in Scripture.

Daniel As "Third in the Kingdom"

Another interesting point relates to Daniel's promotion to third ruler in the kingdom of Babylon (Daniel 5:29). This seemed to be a mistake, for in the Book of Daniel we find that the Babylonian king after Nebuchadnezzar is named Belshazzar (Daniel 5:1). There was no such King Belshazzar, according to the Babylonian lists, and the last Babylonian king was Nabonidus. What was the answer to this problem?

Tablets were eventually found on which were inscribed oaths that Nabonidus took jointly with his son. The two names were linked on the same tablets. Nabonidus was one of Nebuchadnezzar's successors, and we know that he incurred the wrath of the priests of Babylon because for some years he did not even attend the important New Year ceremonies in Babylon. While he was away from the country during those years before Babylon fell, his son Belshazzar acted on his behalf, with full authority as regent. So when we hear of Daniel being made third in the kingdom this is quite accurate, and again shows the local color in the Bible records. Nabonidus, technically, was first, Belshazzar was second, and Daniel was made third when he interpreted the Divine writing on the wall.

The Bible tells us that the children of Judah were permitted to be returned from captivity by the Persian King Cyrus. The Cyrus Cylinder (as it is called) is an interesting parallel account of the incident from the Persian point of view. The Cylinder shows that various peoples were permitted to return to their own land and practice their religion according to their own beliefs. The Bible account (as in Ezra chapter 1) has the Jewish point of view, for the reactions of other peoples were outside the purpose of the Bible writers.

Archaeology Adds To Bible Knowledge

We find that not only are the names of Babylonian kings recorded correctly, but also the names of other kings such as Pharaoh Shishak of Egypt, and various monarchs of Assyria. Perhaps one of the most interesting Assyrian examples was King Sargon, completely unknown except for one reference in Isaiah 20:1. Scholars convincingly argued that this was a Bible error; but then the palace of King Sargon was excavated at Khorsabad, and even the battle described in Isaiah 20 was found recorded in its annals.

Archaeology thus often adds to our Bible knowledge, and sometimes gives us additional facts not contained in the Bible. As an example, we find on what is known as the Moabite Stone that King Omri was so important that a considerable time after he died the people of Moab were still referring to the land of Israel as Omri-land. Omri is dismissed in a few verses in the Bible, for his conduct was unbecoming a king who represented the holy God of Israel. Yet we find from archaeology he was one of the greatest kings Israel ever had, as far as material greatness was concerned. God is not interested in material things, and so Omri (like Jeroboam II some time after him) is dismissed in a few verses in the Bible.

Archaeology also often adds to our knowledge as far as language is concerned. We know that the word "Hanikim" in Genesis 14:14 means "trained servants" or "retainers" because it is known archaeologically between 1,900 B.C. and 1,500 B.C. This term is used only once in the Bible.

Archaeology and the New Testament

One may not realize that archaeology has contributed to our understanding of the New Testament as well as the Old Testament. One should remember the canon of the New Testament covers less than one century, however, compared with many centuries for the Old Testament Scriptures.

The archaeological contribution to our knowledge of the New Testament cannot be over emphasized. One may cite the fragment of papyrus containing parts of John 18:31-33 and 37-38, published in 1935, now in the John Rylands Library in Manchester, England. It dates to about A.D. 125, and so was widely used within a generation of the man who wrote it. It is thought-provoking that this, the earliest fragment of the New Testament, centers around the trial of our Lord, and His own declaration as to His bearing witness to the truth.

Talking Crocodiles

Until the turn of the current century, scholars had debated the nature of New Testament writings — as to whether they were in a special "language of the Holy Spirit." Then in 1899-1900 Drs. B.P. Grenfell and A.S. Hunt, who were excavating in a sacred crocodile cemetery at Tebtunis in the southern Fayum (Egypt), found evidence bearing on this question. The excavations were yielding nothing of value, until a disgusted workman broke open one of the crocodiles. The archaeologists were amazed to see in this and other crocodiles quantities of inscribed papyrus which had been used to stuff the embalmed creatures.

Soon other findings followed, of tremendous significance to New Testament scholarship, for the papyri proved to be everyday documents from Roman times, written in the "koine" Greek of the New Testament. Thus it was demonstrated that the language of the New Testament was the language of "the man in the street" in the 1st century A.D. This is implied in the statement of Mark 12:37: "The common people heard Him gladly."

Luke the Accurate Historian

Possibly the writings of Luke have been challenged more than any other New Testament document. That was all changed, however, by the remarkable researches of Professor Sir William Ransay, one-time Professor of Classical Art at Oxford.

In his work in Asia Minor he needed source material dating to the 1st century A.D., but did not think seriously of Luke, having accepted the Tubingen (German) view that Luke belonged to a later period. But despite his prejudice, Professor Ramsay was eventually to write:

It was gradually borne in upon me that in various details the narrative showed marvellous truth . . . . Luke's history is unsurpassed in respect of its truthworthiness . . . . Luke is an historian of the first rank; not merely are his statements of fact trustworthy; he is possessed of the true historic sense . . . this author should be placed along with the very greatest of historians (*St. Paul the Traveller and the Roman Citizen*).

This accuracy can be demonstrated at many points in the Book of Acts (for Luke wrote *Acts* as well as the Gospel bearing his name). Thus he correctly identifies geographic areas (Acts 13:49; 15:41; 16:2-8); he knows how local officers are described (Acts 13:7; 16:20; 35; 17:6; 18:12; 19:22 and 31); he associates particular deities with certain areas — e.g., Zeus and Hermes at Lystra (Acts 14:11, 12) and Diana at Ephesus (Acts 19:28) — and points up many other aspects which show clearly the touch of first-hand reporting.

The Spiritual Challenge of the Bible

We might mention that Luke, who is so accurate in historical details, has also given us many details of a spiritual nature. This "First-class historian" (as Ramsay called him) has never been proved wrong, and he has been checked at hundreds of points. His seemingly casual references have proved to be signposts clearly pointing to the 1st century A.D. The local color in Luke is conslusive evidence of the genuineness of his writings.

This being the case, it is good reason to accept literally his facts of an essentially spiritual nature. When Luke speaks of the physical resurrection of the Lord Jesus Christ Who "showed Himself alive by many infallible proofs" (Acts 1:3), Luke is not merely an accurate historian — he is a chosen vessel of the Holy Spirit of God to direct us to the Person of Jesus Christ, the Son of God. The Christ is the Savior of all those who accept His salvation by faith, as the gift of God (Acts 1:8; 4:11-12; 16:31).

In this survey, we have seen that archaeology demonstrates the substantial historical value of the Scriptures; it shows that the source documents come from the times of the events they describe; it explains words and customs, and enlarges our knowledge of Bible times, incidents, and happenings; it gives us great confidence in the reliability of the Scriptures, God's Word of Truth.

Clearly we have every right to have confidence in the Bible, despite the way-out theories of Erich von Daniken, the Swiss hotelier turned historian!

11

IS THERE A "DEVIL'S TRIANGLE"?

I was asked to submit my views concerning the controversial geographic area known as "The Devil's Triangle" or "The Bermuda Triangle." I offer this chapter, therefore, as explanation of my views concerning this area, and also wish to state that the examples cited throughout were chosen from among many in defense of my argument.

In my opinion, the best book dealing with the "Devil's Triangle" is *The Bermuda Triangle Mystery Solved* by Lawrence David Kusche (Warner Books, N.Y., $1.95), and what follows leans heavily on Kusche's research. Other "Triangle" books are listed in the bibliography. Their authors would not always agree with Kusche's findings.

"The Bermuda Triangle" consists of an area between Florida, Puerto Rico, and Bermuda. Over the last few years it has received a great deal of attention, partly because of the world-wide phenomena of UFOs and the "mystery" of many disappearances of ships and aircraft in this area, often referred to as "The Devil's Triangle."

The fact is, the so-called "Devil's Triangle" is nothing of the kind, in my opinion. Records have been distorted, and even recent incidents have been magnified into legends with essential facts put to one side. So-called mysteries are not mysteries in the true sense of the word and the number of disappearances in this area is not significantly higher than in other parts of the world.

That does not mean that U.F.O.'s are "out." On the contrary, my book *UFOs., And Their Mission Impossible* gives sufficient reason for believing they are very much "in" — but they are paraphysical entities, with a spiritual explanation that has nothing to do with life on other planets or visits by extra-terrestrial astronauts.

Some Incidents Are Fictional

Lawrence Kusche (see bibliography) has done an excellent job in researching the mystery of the *Rosalie*, a ship which was supposedly found deserted but in perfect order near Nassau, with a half-starved canary the only living creature aboard.

Lloyd's of London do not know anything about a *Rosalie*, but they do know about a *Rossini*. The only reference to the *Rosalie* contemporary with the supposed mystery is in a letter in the *London Times* of November 6, 1840. When the two accounts are put together, it becomes clear that the *Rosalie* was in fact the *Rossini*, and there is no mystery — even though this is one of the "best" stories about the "Bermuda Triangle."

The chart on the following page summarizes two "incidents:"

	London Times, Nov. 6, 1840	Lloyd's List, Sept. 25, 1840
Name of Ship:	*Rosalie*	*Rossini*
Brought into Port:	Nassau (Bahamas)	Nassau
Date into Port:	"Within last few days" — letter dated 27 August, 1840	"Was fallen in with abandoned," 17th ult. (August 1840) and then brought into port as a derelict.
Route being taken:	Hamburg to Havannah	Hambro (Hamburgh) to Havana.
How contact was made:	"Was met by one of small coasters, and was discovered to be completely abandoned."	See above — "was fallen in with abandoned."
Life on board:	A cat, some fowls, several canaries "half-dead with hunger."	No mention, except "abandoned."
Official Records in Nassau	None about *Rosalie*:	Vice-Admiralty Court Minutes concerning Rossini: Reference to "curious circumstances" as to the finding of the *Rossini*.

Official Record About Crew and Passengers

No official record on the crew and passengers exists anywhere concerning *Rosalie*. Lloyd's List of September 25, 1840, says that the *Rossini* struck on the Muare (the Bahama Channel), and that the crew and passengers were saved. The expression "curious circumstances" in the Nassau record indicates that the rescue of the crew and passengers was unknown to the Nassau authorities.

As the above facts are studied it becomes clear that in this case there is no mystery. The ship was the *Rossini*, not the *Rosalie*. It foundered, was abandoned, floated off with a later tide, was boarded and taken into the Port of Nassau, and the crew and passengers were rescued.

To believe otherwise is to suggest an incredible series of coincidences at exactly the same time and even associated with the same port. The mystery is simply the misreporting of a ship's name, and a legend has developed around that one relatively minor error.

Crash Goes "The Devil's Triangle"!

There are other cases where a tradition has developed into legend, having only a fictional basis. One other example is that of the tanker *V.A. Fogg* that supposedly disappeared without any reason or trace on February 1, 1972. The legend is that all 38 of the crewmen disappeared, but that when divers located the wreck on February 14, the captain was found sitting in his cabin with a coffee cup still in his hand.

The facts are that the effects of an explosion were actually witnessed at the time and place of the disappearance when located, reported in *Salveston Daily News* of February 16, 1972. About one-fifth of the tanker had been blown off. Two other bodies besides that of the captain were found, and the captain's body was floating in the chartroom, not seated in his cabin, and he was not holding a coffee cup. In any case, the whole incident was well OUTSIDE the infamous Triangle. Sometimes truth is NOT stranger than fiction!

Many Disappearances Became "Sinister"
Only In Later Reporting

On the night of September 13, 1492, Christopher Columbus noticed that the needle of his ship's compass was pointing about 5 degrees northwest of the North Star. Columbus himself studied the phenomenon for several nights and so did the other ship's pilots. They were at first confused and alarmed, for this variation had never been registered before. However, Columbus came forward with the explanation that the compass did not point to the North Star, but to something else. Because they had confidence in Columbus, the pilots accepted his explanation and their alarm subsided.

Later reporting (especially in this generation!) has exaggerated the panic among the crew, and has made a great deal of this magnetic problem. In fact, it is now well-known that the magnetic north pole is some distance from true north — actually being about half-way between the recognized North Pole and Hudson Bay.

Compasses vary according to particular locations on the earth's surface, and navigators know that they need to make appropriate adjustments. In any case, the "Bermuda Triangle" is not sufficiently close to the North Pole for the variations to be as great as at some other parts of the earth's surface. Sensational writers have made much of supposed magnetic differences in the Triangle area — having their basis in the supposed "sinister" happenings to the compass of Columbus. It makes good reading, but is not an accurate assessment of the facts.

Another "sinister" incident with a "non-sinister" explanation is that of a DC-3 plane that supposedly disappeared mysteriously when in sight of Miami on December 28, 1948. Lawrence Kusche shows (pages 148 ff.) that, in fact, the pilot did not report that he could see the lights of Miami; he merely SAID he was within 50 miles of Miami and could have been mistaken, especially as most of the previous 20 hours had been spent in the air. He and his co-pilot must have been close to exhaustion. The pilot was NOT in touch with the Miami tower, and it is entirely possible that he missed Florida's southern tip and flew off into the Gulf of Mexico, to ditch in the darkness of early evening in a turbulent sea. By the time search planes were in the area next morning, the aircraft could have been forever hidden beneath the waves.

In any case, the aircraft had battery problems before taking off and the transmitter was not working properly. This is made clear in the official report but is omitted in the legend. After all, THAT takes from the mysterious suddenness of the loss of radio contact! Nevertheless, this highly significant fact has been discarded as the legend has grown, and is another example of an incident becoming "sinister" only by later reporting — or, more correctly, misreporting.

Some Incidents Have Been Misreported

There have been various other forms of distortion of the facts. Some incidents have been misreported on such matters as weather conditions. One of the dramatic "without cause" disasters is supposedly that of the Japanese Steamship *Raifuku Maru* which left Boston for Hamburg on April 18, 1925, and the next morning sent out radio messages for help. According to the story, it was a tranquil sea, a totally calm day, and the message for help spoke of trouble "like a dagger — we can't escape." Nothing more was ever heard of the ship or of its crew. Other ships in the area could not explain the mystery.

The facts are that the *Homeric*, a ship of the White Star line, was 70 miles from the Japanese ship and picked up the S.O.S. messages. The last call was, "now very danger. Come quick." The *Homeric* got to the *Raifuku Maru*, but the seas were mountainous. Rescue could not be effected, and the 48 crew members all drowned.

The distortions of the facts are: (1) the weather was not calm, but very heavy; (2) the sea was not tranquil, but "mountainous;" (3) the mysterious word "dagger" was not used, but "danger" was; and (4) other ships could explain the mystery: the *Homeric* actually stood by, helpless to save the crew.

The legend makes for mystery; the facts are rather ordinary. Who wants facts when one can add to an already mysterious legend?

Another misreporting relates to the yacht *La Dahama* which supposedly haunted the Triangle area in August, 1935. According to the tradition, its crew of five was rescued by the Italian liner *Rex* just before the yacht sank, in front of their eyes, on August 27. Five days later the still-floating *La Dahama* was boarded by a landing party from the ship *Aztec*. Apparently, the *La Dahama* had risen from its watery grave!

Actually, the yacht was found by the *Rex* 875 miles north-east of Bermuda, and by the *Aztec* about 700 miles north-east of the same port. Neither of these points was in the "Bermuda Triangle," and the rescued crew did *not* see the yacht sink. The report was that when they were rescued it was in a sinking condition after a five-day storm; but then in a calm sea it drifted for five days before the *Aztec* found it. It was not in the Triangle, nor was there any mystery in the light of the real facts. This was NOT a ghost ship resurrected from the sea!

Those Five Bombers — Human Error,
Night Flying, and Poor Visilibity
Were Contributing Factors

One of the most sensational stories ever told about the "Bermuda Triangle" relates to the mysterious disappearance of five Avenger bombers on December 5, 1945. Then a giant Martin Mariner flying boat, with a crew of 13, took off on a search mission, and it too disappeared.

This story is referred to in my book *U.F.Os. And Their Mission Impossible*. There I relate the rumor that one survivor had been found in a rubber raft, and then I state, "This story about a survivor is not officially substantiated, but it is certain that there is a great mystery associated with the disappearance of those six aircraft and their crews." That was published in the year before Kusche's book, and it seems that here again he has resolved another problem — probably the most sensational of all the supposed "Bermuda Triangle" mysteries.

Kusche analyzes the official reports and reaches a number of conclusions different from those usually put forward. Some of the "popular" parts of the tradition are not in the official record, thus there is no mention of the strange craft closing in, nor of the undue alarm by the tower operators at Miami. The recorded conversations tell of being lost, but there is no great drama in the dialogue. The leader of the flight of bombers was not familiar with the area, and all but one of those with him were trainees. Though they knew they were at times lost, and even disagreed with their leaders as to where they were going, their training meant that they obeyed his orders. The flight changed direction several times, but the flight was never turned over to one of the students because of the leader's panic (as is sometimes claimed). The official report indicates that they were lost for more than four hours and then ran out of fuel, presumably ditching in the sea east of the United States and north of the Bahamas.

Although the weather had been "fair" when the planes took off, it rapidly deteriorated, and this explains the garbled reports and the legend that has developed around the crews' conversations. The search planes reported that the turbulence in the air was extreme and that conditions were unsafe for flying. Very high seas were also reported and this could explain why no debris was ever found. The flight took off at 2:10 p.m., and after various changes of direction, a report came from the leader of the flight at 5:16 p.m., "we will fly 270 (West) until we hit the beach or run out of gas." Then at 5:22 p.m. an order came from Lieutenant Taylor, the leader, "when the first man gets down to ten gallons of gas we will all land in the water together. Does everyone understand that?" Reception kept coming in from the leader until after 7 p.m., long beyond the setting in of darkness. Their fuel supply would have run out about 8 p.m.

Lieutenant Taylor had apparently thought he was over Florida Keys when he was in fact 40 miles north of the Bahamas. He kept asking the time and reported his two compasses as not functioning correctly. Without clock and compass he appears to have become disoriented, and did allow a pilot with a working compass to take the lead position on his instructions. He remained in charge. He declined to change his radio to the emergency channel because he wanted to make sure he kept his flight together. This meant he eventually lost contact with the ground station tracking him.

Very high seas — darkness and poor visibility — acceptance of orders — planes out of gas — with these explanations, much of this mystery is resolved. By the time a daylight search was underway the tempestuous sea would have done its worst, and the five bombers would have been buried beneath the ocean.

What About the Search Plane?

Contrary to the popular tradition, the missing search plane was not the only one sent up, nor was it even the first one. The Mariner took off at 7:27 p.m., and an explosion was reported just where the plane would have been, 23 minutes later. This happened on a dark and stormy night, and not in bright sunlight as the legend would have us believe. Lawrence Kusche states (p. 127) that the Mariners were nicknamed "flying gas tanks" because of fumes, and suggests that a cigarette or a spark could have set off an explosion. Strange coincidences have taken place in history; this loss appears to be another.

Once again, the legend of the "Devil's Triangle" has not stood investigation by impartial observers. I am one writer who has become convinced by the evidence in the official report.

Bad Weather Explains Some Other Incidents

Another supposed victim of evil, supernatural forces in the Triangle area was the steamer *Cotopani* which disappeared in December, 1925, after sailing from Charleston on November 9. *Lloyd's Reports* for December 11, 1925, indicated that the vessel radioed on December 1 that it had water in the hold and was listing badly. The *New York Times* of December 2, 1925, reported that a tempest had paralyzed shipping. It was described by Weather Bureau officials as phenomenal. Many ships had to seek shelter, and massive damage was caused to harbors and cities along the Atlantic coast.

The *Cotopani* was in the path of that storm, as described in the *New York Times*. Despite the tradition, there is no real mystery; the solution is that yet another ship was the victim of the well-known ferocious Atlantic gales. The fact that the ship was in the general area of the Triangle was fortuitous.

Virtually the same explanation can be given for the disappearance of the freighter *Suduffco* that sailed from New Jersey on March 13, 1926, and was due at the Panama Canal about ten days later. She did not arrive, and nothing was ever found of the ship or its 29 crew members, despite a search extending over some weeks. Lawrence Kusche reports (page 89) that the Cunard liner *Aquitania* was approaching New York as the *Suduffco* was leaving. The Captain of the *Aquitania* reported he had come through the worst seas he had ever known, and that the gales holding the ship back had been like tropical cyclones.

Those were the seas into which the *Suduffco* sailed — and Lawrence Kusche has put "SOLVED" against another "Bermuda Triangle" tradition, as the title of his book claims.

Some "Triangle" Disappearances Might Have Been Elsewhere

It is also true that sensational reporting (including book-writing) has tended to give credit to the "Bermuda Triangle" for disappearances that possibly have nothing to do with that area. A good example is the British Navy training ship the *Atalanta*. It sailed for England from Bermuda on January 31, 1880, and was not heard from again.

Popular tradition has linked this with the "Devil's Triangle" and supernatural "snatching," but two points should be stressed. One is that severe storms wracked the Atlantic Ocean along the course to be taken by the *Atalanta*, and a considerable amount of debris was sighted in the two months after the ship sailed; some of it might have been from the *Atalanta*. Secondly, the projected voyage was of approximately 3,000 miles, and only 500 miles lay in the area of the Triangle. The ship could have foundered anywhere between Bermuda and England.

That spoils the story of course — so it *must* have been a victim of the "Devil's Triangle." Or was it?

Another case is that of the small German ship the *Freya*, found deserted at sea on October 20, 1902. Its point of departure was listed in Lloyd's Register as Manzanillo, and therein lies the probability that the *Freya* did *not* meet disaster in the "Bermuda Triangle." An article in *Nature*, dated April 25, 1907, discusses a famous Mexican earthquake with effects stretching out into the Pacific Ocean. It elaborates the tragedy of the *Freya* that left Manzanillo on October 3, 1902, for Punta Arenas on the southern tip of South America. Twenty days later it was found lying on its side, partially dismasted, near Mazatlan. Weather conditions had been good, but there were earthquakes on October 4 and 5 — the captain's wall calendar showed the last date as October 4.

This article refers to the cities of Manzanillo, Acapulco, and Chilpanzuigo, all of which are on the west side of Mexico — the Pacific side. In other words, the ship was associated with Manzanillo, the west coast of Mexico, and not with Manzanillo in the "Bermuda Triangle," on the east side of America. The sameness of name has caused another tragedy to be wrongly linked with the "Devil's Triangle."

Some "Incidents" Not Even Near "The Bermuda Triangle!"

As the tradition about the Triangle has grown, it

has included a number of disappearances well outside the area.

The ship *Bella* is in this category. It left Rio de Janeiro in April, 1845, and completed only 6 days of its voyage to Jamaica. When its ship's boat was found, floating upside down, it was many hundreds of miles south of the "Bermuda Triangle." Even with the most favorable conditions the overloaded *Bella* would have been considerably less than halfway toward its destination of Jamaica. Its disappearance had nothing to do with the supposed peculiarities of the "Bermuda Triangle" despite its "adoption" into the Triangle legend.

Similarly, the U.S. Air Force globemaster that disappeared with 53 men on board on March 23,1951, was on the way to the British Isles. Evidence of a probable explosion was found, and the incident occurred at a great distance from the "Bermuda Triangle," despite the legend claiming this also "as one of its own."

A British troop transport plane was lost on February 2, 1953, with 39 persons on board. There was a severe storm over the Atlantic at the time, and was the apparent cause of this tragic incident. However, contrary to the tradition, the incident occurred some 900 miles north of the Triangle.

Various other cases could be cited. The fact is, the legend of "The Bermuda Triangle" continues to demand cases to support the theory. Why worry about a few hundred miles here and there?

Not all the disappearances in the "Bermuda Triangle" have been resolved, nor have they been resolved in various other places across the earth's surface. However, as this chapter indicates, enough answers are forthcoming to show that "The Devil's Triangle" is a misnomer for the so-called "Bermuda Triangle."

CONCLUSION

We do not discount the mysterious, and we readily acknowledge that startling knowledge was demonstrated in the construction of the pyramids and many other ancient buildings.

However, such capacities are not really surprising. Although they are at times beyond our knowledge, that certainly does not mean we must look for the explanations by calling up visitors from outer space. Lost techniques have a habit of proving to be rather simple when the explanation is eventually known.

A simple illustration is relevant. When I was Director of the Australian Institute of Archaeology, I had occasion to have a bronze piece mended. It dated to about 1500 B.C., and the metallurgist who supervised the work told me they did not know how the original piece was cast. The bronze was harder than was known in modern times. Recently I met that same man and reminded him of the incident. Now I found that in the intervening years the process had become understood, because the techniques had been utilized in making Japanese Samurai swords. First they were flattened to paper thinness, then beaten back the other way. This was repeated several times, and in the process the steel acquired a new hardness. Once again an ancient process had given up its secret to modern research.

Another relevant point, often overlooked, is that "ancient" men were much nearer to creation. If early men did live for great periods of time, even apart from the Bible there is good reason to believe this, then in some areas their knowledge is likely to be significantly greater than that of twentieth century man. Man has always been a highly intelligent being, right from his creation "in the image of God." It is not really surprising that sometimes our ancestors had a knowledge beyond our own. That knowledge had its origin in God Himself. He made man in His own image. The cognitive processes of early man have not been improved, though his technical skill has been developed.

The answer to the mysteries of the past does not lie with visiting spacemen, conveniently contacting man at the right psychological moment. The answer lies in the intelligence of man, for even fallen man still retained a potential dramatically superior to that of the most intelligent non-human being.

We have seen in this book that those gods in their chariots continue to crash in the mounds of antiquity.

more significant books for you...

EVOLUTION? The Fossils Say NO!
Duane T. Gish

The fossil record provides the critical evidence for or against evolution since no other scientific evidence can show the actual history of living things. The fossil record proves there has been no evolution in the past and none in the present. This important fact is conclusively documented by Dr. Gish in this critique of the evolutionary philosophy. 134 pages, Quality Paperback.

Scientific Creationism   *Henry M. Morris, Editor*

An honest understanding of man and his world can only be acquired from accurate information. This valuable and wholly scientific handbook covers the subjects of origins and early earth history, and the entire field of the creationist alternative to evolution. Often used as a textbook for the study of origins. General Edition, *Includes Biblical Documentation.* 277 pages, Kivar; or Cloth. Public School Edition, *Non-Religious Text.* 217 pages, Kivar; or Cloth.

The Troubled Waters of Evolution
Henry M. Morris

The theory of evolution is a delusion and cannot be supported by the facts of science. It is a humanistic philosophy which requires more faith on the part of the believer than does belief in biblical creationism. Dr. Morris presents evolution as it is, an unsound scientific concept which has yet to be proven. Concerned and thinking people in all walks of life will want to read this controversial, revealing new book. 217 pages, Quality Paperback.

The Bible's Influence on American History
Tim F. LaHaye

An eloquent, concise presentation of the influence the Bible has had on American History and how it can affect our future if we let it. The content and special line drawings make it a fine gift book. 96 pages, Paper.

Many Infallible Proofs *Henry M. Morris*

A comprehensive and systematic handbook written as a survey of the unique truth and authority of biblical Christianity. Contains evidence from science, prophecy, history, internal structure, philosophy and common sense. Complete with questions and answers, an excellent reference for church and home study. 381 pages: Kivar, Cloth, or book and cassette Set.

The Remarkable Birth of Planet Earth
Henry M. Morris

An exciting journey back to our beginnings is in this concise introductory treatment of origins. Covers the amazing order of the universe, early history of all mankind, delusion of evolution, the worldwide flood and many other historical and prophetic confirmations of God's handiwork. 111 pages, Paper.

The Genesis Record
A Scientific and Devotional Commentary
on the Book of Beginnings
Henry M. Morris

Written as a narrative exposition, The Genesis Record is the only commentary on the complete book of Genesis written by a creationist scientist. Discussions on all important historical and scientific problems are woven into the narrative which holds the interest of the reader throughout. Convincing treatments are given to the record of an actual six-day special creation, the worldwide flood, the dispersion, and the lives of the patriarchs exactly as written in Genesis. 708 Pages, Cloth.

The Bible Has the Answer
Revised and enlarged
Henry M. Morris and Martin Clark

Bible answers to puzzling questions on the Bible-science, doctrine, Christian life, and behavior and relationships. Now you can have Bible-centered answers to the 150 most common and vexing questions on the Bible and the Christian life. About 400 pages, Quality Paperback.

Crash Go the Chariots
Clifford Wilson

Newly revised and enlarged, the original book of this title was the near million bestselling answer to von Daniken's theories concerning unexplained happenings and ruins. These revealing answers to mysterious and haunting questions will arouse your curiosity and at the same time provide sensible answers to von Daniken and his often absurd claims. About 156 pages, Paper.

East Meets West in
THE OCCULT EXPLOSION *Clifford Wilson*

Pagan and semi-religious movements are now sweeping Western culture with unusually successful results in securing converts. Spiritism, witchcraft, and other Satanic cults are on the one hand, and transcendental meditation, yoga, Hare Krishna and other eastern philosophic movements are springing up on the other hand. This evaluation is very timely and has real help for these very confusing times when Satanic power is being felt more than at any other time in history. About 156 pages, Paper.

Adventure on Ararat
John D. Morris

Mysterious, foreboding, unexplored Ararat! Will anyone ever discover the secrets of this majestic mountain? John Morris and others searched for Noah's Ark on this awesome mountain and kept a diary of their trip. Now you can read about this expedition with the many unexpected trials they encountered. 116 pages, Quality Paperback.

THE ARK ON ARARAT: the Search Goes On
Tim F. LaHaye and John D. Morris

The most complete and up-to-date exposition of all that is known about Noah's Ark, its modern sightings, and future prospects for discovery. Fully illustrated with beautiful color photographs. You can actually join the search if you desire with the section on things which you can do to help locate the Ark. 288 Pages, Quality Paperback.

Creation: Acts/Facts/Impacts, Vol. I

*Edited by Henry M. Morris, Duane T. Gish,
George M. Hillestad*

The Institute for Creation Research issues a monthly publication entitled "Acts and Facts" which carries articles about creationism and the work of the Institute in seminars, debates, and special meetings. This book is a compilation of important articles from June, 1972, through December, 1973, plus the entire "Impact" series no. 1 - no. 9. 193 pages, Quality Paperback.

Creation: Acts/Facts/Impacts, Vol. II

Edited by Henry M. Morris and Duane T. Gish

The revival of creationism continues and becomes more exciting each year. This volume contains articles of continuing interest from the Institute for Creation Research as published in their monthly Acts and Facts during 1974 and 1975. About 250 pages, Quality Paperback.

Has God Spoken?

A. O. Schnabel

God has given man ample evidence of His existence, His nature, and His communication with men through the ages. The purpose of this study is to accredit the testimony of the writers of this record, the Bible. 119 pages, Quality Paperback.